Thinking the Unthinkable, In Pursuit of Sound Money

"Money without limit creates problems without solution. Money should be limited in nature"

22nd Feb 2016

Accepted thought acknowledges that power corrupts and absolute power corrupts absolutely. As Thomas Jefferson said there is nothing more powerful than control of the money, "banks are more dangerous to our liberties than standing armies". What is used as the means of exchange and how it's perceived, sets off a chain of events, like the flapping wings of the butterfly, forming what we know as society. It is the keystone containing all our values and desires. It encapsulates and controls all aspects of our lives, the power to create or control it, is the absolute power and therefore liable to absolute corruption.

For the past year I have tried to explain why the money we use is so important to society, that money is a constant in almost all matters and at its heart contains the values of those who have used it. Ever since the barter system, how the money is organised determines the "values and moral priorities" of those using it. Generally, if the money is unsound it is spent or exchanged; if it is sound it is kept and saved. Fiat money in use today is fundamentally unsound and unsustainable because it is created and unlimited. I will explain how it is based on a classic pyramid scheme, sustained only by illusion and deception, designed to funnel real assets to the top, creating widening inequality and distorting time itself as activity is conjured up from the future. It is the root cause of the widely accepted regression that society is experiencing yet the majority of people don't know where money comes from, who controls it, and how it shapes the moral values and lives of everyone who use it.

"The truth has a ring which ripples through closed doors and sheltered minds."

The Government of the most powerful country on earth is a special case worth noting. In less than a generation the US has conducted endless war for the military industrial complex, revenge and oil, then against ideology, destroying the Constitution in the process, created a total surveillance state conducted through panopticon technology, and that's ignoring a complete financial system bailout by The Federal Reserve Bank which is accountable to nobody on earth. Even on that brief pastiche it is a trend which needs reversing. Only sound money can help reinstate the Constitution and put the US Government back on track.

In the not so distant past gold was universally accepted as the true measure of value. It was limited in nature. Today, with nuclear weapons and ensured destruction, the established order of countries is more permanent. Nuclear weapons changed the political landscape forever. Wars will now only ever be local skirmishes. World Wars could never happen in a fight for sources of gold or other treasure because nobody would fight for them knowing victory was impossible as the ultimate destruction would be used in the face of defeat. Nuclear weapons were true game changers.

To prevent the intellectual, moral and physical corruption of absolute power, the power to create money, those who wield it should be accountable. That something, that universal belief, that truth, that God, should be nature itself. Our money should be limited in nature, something everybody can understand and believe in. Money which is limited forces governments to act responsibly, to act in accordance with nature, to focus on the possible instead of just conjuring with words. It holds those with power to account, keeping them connected to the powerful rhythms of nature.

For me, the solution is clear; we must decide what we value in nature and limit the money to that so that those charged with supplying it remain grounded and responsible.

Over the last year, I have used the comments section of the mainstream media to post all my minded thoughts on various subject matters, mostly money, economics and politics, expressing to the readers, and hopefully those in power, those who don't want to be accountable in nature, to consider the possibility that alternatives exist. I've tried to use everything I could find in the pantechnicon and armed with the greatest language on earth, I have made my pitch. I hope you enjoy the thought experiment. It may be an ill-favoured thing but it's my own.

The sinister treatment of dissent at the BBC

9 Mar 2015 09:57

Who is working for who? The BBC looks like the PR department for HSBC and as a result, the stated goal of trust and impartiality is being smashed on the rocks.

I'm sure she's a lovely lady but "Rona Fairhead, HSBC and the BBC" should be the biggest story of the decade so far, on a par with "who killed Lucy Beale in EastEnders " and that was covered like it was Black Caviar by Frankel.

BBC News requires a caveat emptor health warning.

Rona Fairhead should lose BBC job over HSBC role, says influential MP

10 Mar 2015 10:41

We are all signalling all of the time.

When the BBC trot out a specimen from Freud's everybody should be able to read the signs.

A new broom urgently required.

Tweed and local insight are key to a successful Cheltenham Gold Cup

14 Mar 2015 13:11

I thought it was a good article.

This year I watched the Festival in the mirror, sorry the TV, it looked emotional. The only antidote to that is pure thought, to see beauty and the right of the thing without desire.

For me, the highlight was obviously Coneygree but the Scudamore's touching off Ireland for the Prestbury Cup was a sensational result all round.

Grant Shapps: just how gullible does he think voters are?

16 Mar 2015 17:34

Who is the PM going to bag?

As I see it the BBC beaters have flushed out Grant Shapps towards Mr Cameron's gun. He has double barrels but 3 birds to choose from, what will he do? It's all up in the air but I suspect "big bird

Clarkson" being quite popular and probably flying very low may be the hardest shot.

A bumpy ride awaits the SNP on Westminster's see-saw

30 Mar 2015 11:02

Britain's political weakness is obvious, a gaping hole of a problem. The leader of the SNP is an unreasonable woman and she proves that men don't have a monopoly on hubris, arrogance and poor judgement. At least Alec Salmond only wanted Independence.

Proposing a 50p tax rate on the whole of Britain is over steeping the mark. Her ambitions have taken a couple of months to get out of hand simply because she wants to be Queen Bee. I call on Alec to retake control of her condition and the SNP so we can all work together for friends on both sides of the Border. If Alec wants to discuss this over a round of golf I would be happy to take £40 off him in a scratch game.

Whoever wins Hove … on the election trail in the bellwether seat

30 Mar 2015 10:25

A Triptych of the Polls and the Political Marketplace

Pollsters are merely weather makers, tipsters and touts with vested interests. The market is so much more than that, the aggregation of all minded thoughts backed up by cold hard cash. Sometimes the market maybe wrong but over the march of time it will always contain the truth. I'd follow a free market every every every time.

For my money, the election outcome will be made, as always, on the margins; north, south, east and west where disparate positions and views collide, a political Hadron Collider. In these environments volatility is higher as people search for the "path of least resistance" where they can balance cui bono and social responsibility. Influences may come from many sources, such as local press, national press, the Google brain, personal prejudice, local influencers, family, and friends – from all interactions in people's daily lives. When all is said and done a market, especially a free one, will always take the path of least resistance.

Boris Johnson: 'Vote Tory, get broadband. Vote Ukip, get Miliband'

1 Apr 2015 16:32

In response to Galaxina

The plan is getting the UK's finances back under control by balancing the budget. This in turn shores up the currency and reduces our exposure to being turned over in the money markets because of the huge debt burden caused by Blair and Brown.

As a country we have taken a lead and you can see the results, just look at the state of Europe.

1 Apr 2015 14:42

I have more interest in my cup of tea than Boris Johnson but this article does highlight a interesting point.

Nobody in their right mind will trust Labour with the money and economy but many distrust the Conservatives as heartless corporate sociopaths. For me, the Conservatives have the right economic plan but need to show they have a heart.

If the Conservatives pledged to move with speed to legislate over the next parliament to increase the minimum wage towards a living wage, thousands and thousands of unregistered and undecided voters would flock to the polls for a Conservative majority.

Raising the "water line" would serve many masters. Businesses who are already plumbing the depths with questionable business plans would bleat but with all new certainties they would quickly adapt.

The increased labour costs would eventually be passed through the supply chain into higher aggregate prices. All of the increase in wages would be spent by the individuals but the major beneficiary would be Mr Carney and his inflation target which is teetering on the brink. Mr Carney and the Treasury would be doing hand stands as the inflation trend is re-established in the nation's calculations.

Revealed: the winner of the leaders' election debate

3 Apr 2015 08:49

Most people wont bet on a horse race without a racecard. For my money, it was a kindergarten level debate with an air of farce, even the presenter changed blinkers mid race, totally ungenuine. Only Mr Farage and the PM had a grasp of the problem.

Side bets: Rupert Murdoch's YouGov took 2 minutes to poll 500 people to determine the debate result, what a nonsense. Conclusion: Voters want to back a genuine animal not a show pony as leader.

How the subconscious mind shapes creative writing

7 Apr 2015 12:28

For me, only music and the written word can talk to the heart, whereas visual images are merely a reflection on the soul.

Real, Classical Art is the ability to talk without words.

Boris Johnson isn't the magic bullet the Tories imagine

10 Apr 2015 09:59

To my mind, Boris Johnson is the epitome of Tory arrogance and hypocrisy, he reminds me of the old maxim " the privileged born foolish care not for their state"

Tory austerity will eat up the welfare state

13 Apr 2015 10:03

I wish someone would ask these incompetent deficit denying socialist politicians the following question: "If money is just a printed piece of paper with a number on it, why don't we chop down the trees and we can all be rich?"

Running a balanced budget is the only way of sustaining this system, the soundness of our money, and reducing inequality. The rich (people and businesses) will have to pay more in tax.

Don't forget fiat economics is a global game of Paper,scissors, stone and at the moment the world is beholden to the US and the Fed.

Paper- paper money
Scissors- the strength of the argument against it
Stone- the army required to protect the fiat/paper money system

What difference does Labour's 'budget responsibility lock' make?

14 Apr 2015 08:50

Labour still have debt issues.

The fact Labour can't admit they want to borrow £30bn a year just conveys, to anyone listening, that they have no confidence in their own plan.

Lib Dems will not enter Tory coalition if £12bn welfare cuts made – Nick Clegg

14 Apr 2015 08:56

Nick Clegg is an insufferable power crazed fool without a plan, apart from dreaming of becoming the next William of Orange.

IMF forecast blows hole in George Osborne's deficit reduction plan

16 Apr 2015 09:43

The IMF are a bell-weather for inaccurate forecasts primarily because they are elitist and believe in trickle down economics and fiat money.

It seems clear that trickle down economics is blocked and a new vision is needed. If we can remove the obstructions of unsound money and the resulting corporate and institutional greed and corruption we can create a bubbling stream of ideas and good will bounded by lush greens banks teaming with wildlife.

The stream flows into the sea which rains on the hills and feeds the stream, a natural cycle in perfect balance.

Miliband tells Sturgeon in final TV debate: I won't do a deal with you

17 Apr 2015 10:35

In response to belvedere

Sharpen up, the BBC don't employ pollsters or advisors unless they know what advice they will be given.

17 Apr 2015 09:43

For me, the BBC got the result they wanted.

Ed Miliband won the debate by a distance, Leanne Wood seemed fixated on having a finger on the button, Nigel Farage verged on the offensive, Natalie Bennett was very keen on being humane and Nicola Sturgeon was the archetypal one-trick pony.

What worries me is that the BBC's default decision is always to dumb down, they desperately need some new friends, all of it symptomatic of the wider malaise.

Nick Clegg urges Scots to vote tactically to keep out SNP

17 Apr 2015 18:06

Another underwhelming glimpse inside Nick Clegg's abandoned barn of ideas.

Why don't they have people like Miranda Green standing for Parliament, she would be Lib Dem leader in a matter of months.

Tottenham condemn Newcastle to sixth straight defeat

20 Apr 2015 08:32

The well organised fan boycott left Ashely's Sports Direct/Wonga stadium naked. He is quickly challenging Jimmy Saville as Britain's most hated man, although like all sociopaths, I doubt he cares.

Martin Rowson on Tory economic policy – cartoon

21 Apr 2015 13:40

Dismiss the economics at your peril. Although its not covered by the Guardian or BBC, 3 Month Euribor went negative today for the 1st time ever.

Just for clarity, that means Mr Draghi's QE has resulted in banks being paid to borrow.

In our brave new world - free money just got cheaper

Nicola Sturgeon challenged on spending plans as SNP backs Labour on tax

21 Apr 2015 09:21

I can't believe the word of Nicola Sturgeon and her barmy army are taken so seriously.

Yesterday she claimed she's not a betting person, which is astonishing considering what she's trying to do.

Her soft soap doesn't wash with me.

Ed Miliband's slow walk to cool

21 Apr 2015 10:54

One of the worst articles I've ever read in the Guardian, I bet the author is the type to like a selfie, someone who thinks they are "capturing the moment" but really they are missing the moment itself.

Labour still don't get it, they would be trusted to carry out the fairness bit but people worry about the profligate money bit, the extra spending, borrowing and taxing. If they could sort out their monetary issues they would win by a street, but they can't. A long-held mistaken ideology is a hard condition to escape from.

In Ed Miliband's case it's all about up holding his father's legacy, a Marxist chalice.

The speed camera never lies

26 Apr 2015 11:57

Of all the subjects in all the world, poor Victoria seems to have been corralled into a prison of her own cognizance, although they do say that marriage is a trap that nobody returns.

Labour's rent control plans explained

26 Apr 2015 17:35

"Rent Control" is a policy with the right sentiment but with awful execution. They are signalling they want rental prices down but don't have the balls to be honest about it.

Literally an ironic position.

Will scrapping stamp duty for first-time buyers push up house prices?

27 Apr 2015 14:05

This stamp duty proposal is just tinkering around the problem. The real issue for me is Labour's dangerous borrowing plans and here is why.

Government borrowing (selling bonds) is not the same as individual or corporate borrowing. Individuals have to pay their loans back, governments generally roll theirs, and if they have to roll over at higher rates it can't be afforded (especially when you've already got a huge debt pile).

It really is as simple as that.

Top economist attacks Tory austerity – and Labour's limp response

29 Apr 2015 09:24

Trotting out Mr Krugman is a sure sign of desperation and a lost argument.

The keynesians want you ignorant but healthy, its tantamount to saying: don't bother growing up, your future has already been spent.

Shock stalling of US economy hits chances of early Fed rate rise

30 Apr 2015 09:30

Mrs Yellen's Fed look to be in disarray

If Russell Brand is pushing 40, who represents the actual youth?

30 Apr 2015 09:24

I was surprised Ed Miliband left Russell Brand's shag palace, I'm sure his wife was relieved

Ronnie O'Sullivan knocked out of World Championship by Stuart Bingham

30 Apr 2015 09:26

The pink and brown cost O'Sullivan another world title

BBC defends Question Time over claims of audience 'bias'

30 Apr 2015 12:08

If history is any guide I expect the BBC to deliver another dose of pro-Labour poison flour

Ed Miliband: I won't have Labour government if it means deals with SNP

1 May 2015 11:53

As I saw it, the BBC held a fair race which the PM won by a clear head from a surprisingly good run by Nick Clegg. Ed Miliband trailed in ahead of Nicola Sturgeon, Leanne Wood and the bankers buddy, Nigel Farage. If you promise not to tell anyone, I've bet the house on a new Conservative Liberal coalition.

Ed Miliband on the 'arrogance of power', junk food and fairness

5 May 2015 16:49

As the Reuters columnist James Saft wrote today "the world is becoming bigger, not smaller, it is de-globalising." He may well be right, but one thing is certain, the Labour party continue to hold onto outdated ideology and dogma.

For example, they continue to conflate wealth with debt (as yesterday's Guardian piece about David Lammy so eloquently exposed). Ed Miliband and the SNP barmy army believe debt is wealth, whereas others understand debt is merely an instrument to borrow, which as we've already seen, can be extremely dangerous. Under a fiat system, which Ed Balls and Miliband so heartily endorse, cui bono and narcissism is king, under progressive sound monetary policies, society and the greater good is king. Perversely, Labour want to continue the debt, borrowing and taxing which caused the problems and suffering in the 1st place.

That is why voting Labour is misguided and dangerous for the good of all not just a few.

Calais: Britain willing to send more security assistance, says Cameron

24 Jun 2015 16:48

This fiasco is hardly surprising when so many on the continent think Britain is the howling mad dog of Europe. The BBC and Government in collaboration with the Banks have been conducting a deviant petri dish experiment in hypocrisy and central planning on the British population, namely to gamble the entire country, including every individual in it, on a debt ladened housing market. A debt fuelled bubble with a fiat currency, which guarantees two scenario's:

a) rampant and rising inequality and inter-generational impoverishment or
b) a bubble popping financial crash.

Both scenarios are fundamentally insecure, unsustainable and are discussed in the new book "Propaganda in the 21st Century" available on Amazon.

What a state of affairs, to create an economic proposition, for individuals, of mutually assured destruction, the Americans call it MAD. For 40 years, this economic noose of financial enslavement has left the public either in a state of denial or they are understandably depressed by the situation engineered for them.

Everything the BBC and the Government now does is to preserve and control the conditions in the Petri dish that is the UK property bubble. It also explains why being a politician is a fundamentally dishonest profession. To prevent or delay the likelihood of scenario b) successive governments, mostly Blair and Brown, opened the flood gates to immigration with the intention of:

1) stoking the demand side of the housing equation and
2) depress wage inflation thereby reducing the pressure on interest rates.

Unfortunately, central planners made a huge tactical and intellectual error in allowing millions of migrants into the country carrying the ideology of Islam and the desire for Sharia law. With hindsight we know Sharia Law is incompatible in a country with a Judeo-Christian history, at the very least because they want to ban interest on money.

Real leadership is now required and the age of politicians lying, deceiving and obfuscating around the truth of the situation must come to an end. Politicians must tell the truth with the truth despite it being unpalatable with the general public because as you can see, the truth is a slippery thing, which needs genuine honesty and care to handle.

Harriet Harman attacks David Cameron over tax credit cuts and pay levels

25 Jun 2015 10:21

Women walk the streets fisting their handbags but Harriet Harman seems unable to lay a glove on the PM.

How hard can it be for a politician to say the words....

Why don't we bring back the Gold Standard? or
Why don't we discuss the process of money creation? or
Why don't we raise interest rates so we can start saving again?

She might get a better response if she did.

The Libertines at Glastonbury 2015 review – whimsical nostalgia

27 Jun 2015 08:46

Glastonbury and its pyramid scheme stage is now just a thinly veiled license to print money - no surprise the BBC are crawling all over it.

Greece debt crisis: Athens fails to repay IMF as bailout runs out - as it happened

30 Jun 2015 08:54

Such slippery weather, in the cradle of democracy.

For the average Greek citizen the choice should be clear, they should default, leave the Euro, remain within the EU and reinstate the Drachma. Within a couple of years they will be in a far stronger position.

The most vulnerable position is held by the EU and the ECB who are trying to maintain a monetary union without a fiscal one.

At the end of the day it will be time for Greece to decide whether it's European or Greek. It will choose to be Greek over European every time.

The BBC is under threat because its success challenges market ideology

30 Jun 2015 10:08

The good thing about Polly Toynbee is that she is consistently wrong

Greece awaits ECB decision on emergency aid

1 Jul 2015 12:10

The mainstream media, led by the BBC, continue to conflate Debt with Wealth..... Greece must accept a bailout to stay afloat.

In reality, the Greek boat would be a lot lighter without the Weight of Debt.

Facebook boss Mark Zuckerberg thinks telepathy tech is on its way

1 Jul 2015 12:00

An interesting article which conveys clearly that Zuckerborg holds some extreme views.

If only people knew that TWITTER and FACEBOOK is just a thinly veiled intelligence file which citizens dutifully update of their own volition. I find it staggering given governments recent track record in decision making.

People have become so docile and accepting despite evidence of rank hypocrisy and cronyism all around in plain view, exemplified by the likes of HSBC's Rona Fairhead as head of the BBC trust.

Google frees its dream robots to run wild across the internet

4 Jul 2015 08:45

people should declare force majeure on google

Greek debt crisis: referendum to go ahead as court rejects appeal

3 Jul 2015 16:33

Intelligent Greeks should leave the Euro.

If I were Hillary Clinton, I'd rather Cherie Blair just left me alone

3 Jul 2015 15:30

Cronyism is insidious and she is a leader in her field

Osborne accuses BBC of 'imperial ambitions' and calls for savings

5 Jul 2015 14:45

The BBC is run by HSBC whichever way you look at it.

Bad banks must fail, good one's must survive.

Eurozone tells Greece not to expect debt relief in near future

7 Jul 2015 10:25

The referendum has backfired for Count Draghi so the ECB is reverting back to type and continuing to mine the pit of future problems. Can Mrs Merkel control him this time?

The moment of truth: can vibrant new England survive Australia onslaught?

8 Jul 2015 08:51

Have the Aussies come with a tower of chips or stable stack?

Mitchell Johnson's action look decidedly crook to me.

The Guardian view on the BBC deal: it could jeopardise, rather than underpin, public support

8 Jul 2015 09:28

The levee is overgrown with weeds and dead wood. The Reds at the BBC must go and Liberty and Democracy must stay.

Serena Williams v Maria Sharapova: a rivalry threatens to catch fire

9 Jul 2015 08:06

Sharapova has all the grace of a good Gloucester Old Spot.

Everyone can see there is nothing behind her grunt apart from frustration.

China bans major shareholders from selling their stakes for next six months

9 Jul 2015 08:44

Under the Fiat $ everything the world does, apart from true love, is predicated on deceit.

We are living in a dystopian world of the central planner where money has no value and all markets are fixed to the point of farce.

The BBC News Channel must be saved

9 Jul 2015 15:53

HSBBC is a fertile breeding ground for questionable judgement and morality, bent on the destruction of the future with unsound money and bad banks.

HSBBC need to have a good look round on their isolated farm and see the lie of the land, which fences have they maintained, with pathways have they kept clear, and most importantly which banks have they kept clean? To me the levee looks overgrown with weeds and deadwood.

The evidence suggests some leaders in HSBBC dream of a Marxist technocracy backed by fiat money and rapacious banks but most people just want Liberty complimented with Democracy.

When all is said and done, the HSBBC farm produces expensive and poor quality produce in an unsustainable manner.

BBC to ask over-75s to pay licence fee voluntarily to offset 10% budget cut

10 Jul 2015 12:18

The BBC have dropped another Clanger.

Top Tory leads rebellion against relaxation of foxhunting ban

12 Jul 2015 11:00

Cityfolk believe the fox represents the citizen hunted by the establishment. In reality countryfolk know it is quite the reverse.

The fox represents a rapacious and plundering government which, as Thomas Jefferson remarked, needs to be limited to maintain liberty.

Voting yes for fox hunting is voting yes for good governance.

Why the eurozone crisis is just part of our long struggle for peace

12 Jul 2015 10:47

Mrs Yellen's shrill is wrong.

The world is in the thrall of the fiat US dollar and mutually assured destruction. Unsound money is holding the world to ransom without the arguments to back it up.

Money with no value has zero interest rates, yet the Fed appears mute on the subject.

The BBC is perfectly set up for future challenges

12 Jul 2015 19:49

Tony Hall is doing a great job if you like cronyism, incompetence and lack of leadership.

Tsipras faces clash with Syriza radicals opposed to eurozone bailout for Greece

13 Jul 2015 14:06

In the protectorate formally known as the Hellenic Republic of Greece, Mr Tispras has voluntarily jumped into the hangman's noose, cowardly choosing **certain death over a chance at life.**

Surely intelligent Greeks will not stand for that?

With her comments on the benefits cap, Harriet Harman is voicing a Tory agenda

13 Jul 2015 11:04

The problem with Labour is they still wear Blair's "daisy chain of mistakes" with pride.

BBC fights back against Tory assault on 'waste' and right to make popular shows

14 Jul 2015 09:00

It's obvious Rona Fairhead and Tony Hall don't like to give out but the fundamental issue is they need to stop conflating debt with wealth. It is like selling torture as democracy.

Debt is not wealth and to continue selling rotten apples to the public makes the BBC fundamentally unsound.

Greek debt crisis: Tsipras vows not to 'abandon ship'; IMF urges massive debt relief - as it happened

14 Jul 2015 09:11

The ECB is offering Greece a tres usury deal.

Interest rate hike is moving closer, Bank of England governor tells MPs

14 Jul 2015 14:10

The Treasury Committee was littered with clangers and not a squeak about the real issue of fiat economics and the metaphorical loaded gun (now with hollow points) held by Mrs Yellen to the head of the world.

Wage bill for BBC's top earners rises by a fifth

14 Jul 2015 20:45

The BBC are great at what they do; tell mostly terrible stories to "citizens" they consider to be uninformed, uneducated and bored.

That said, I do enjoy watching Jeremy Paxman rear up on University Challenge.

The government's witch-hunters are ready to reform the BBC to death

19 Jul 2015 11:28

Stewart Lee is entirely prejudiced as HSBBC is his mobility scooter allowing him to spend Monday afternoon's in Wetherspoon creeping out the bar staff and urinating on the toilet floor.

Jordan Spieth misses out on three in a row but still has stake in history

21 Jul 2015 15:20

Jordon Spieth tries to putt ahead of time, the problem with that is the future has already been spent.

BBC is one of the UK's greatest assets, says Arts Council chair

21 Jul 2015 17:48

I'm sorry but that's toilet, the BBC is a howling mad dog Keynesian Marxist which ignores the fact that governments do not have a good track record in paying their debts back.

They have sold out to the illusion of unsound fiat money and must be set free and allowed to compete.

Crikey! Boris Johnson isn't PM material after all

22 Jul 2015 10:29

Boris Johnson is the embodiment of the truism:

"the privileged born foolish care not for their state"

Peers put brakes on government's plans for English votes for English laws

22 Jul 2015 11:05

This story is emblematic of the wider malaise which starts with the Oxford and Cambridge feeder school of government, a brace of fat cock hens strutting around the manor producing the foul arguments that ultimately populate the House of Lords and BBC etal, whose job is to conceal the truth about the Fed's fiat dollar and our consequent enslavement.

Donald Trump reveals Republican rival Lindsey Graham's phone number on TV

22 Jul 2015 10:10

In my humble opinion, the British should ride into Washington with our winning arguments, but this time in blue coats, and set the US Government free from the Fed's fiat dollar.

Blair condemns Corbyn as Corbyn sets out his economic policies - Politics live

22 Jul 2015 11:10

Blair sounds desperate, tired and emotional, I'm surprised he didn't claim the Nazi gold is in Rolex.

Enid Blyton's cottage goes on sale

22 Jul 2015 15:47

I am very sceptical about children's fantasy books because they are designed to acclimatise the young mind to illusions and make believe which they are supposed to believe in when they grow up, such as rampant property bubbles and a financial system based on a pyramid scheme of debt.

BBC Trust: licence fee should not be replaced by subscription

22 Jul 2015 15:54

The HSBBC, like Jimmy Savile, want to dance with who they like when they like.

They risk becoming a flaccid organisation just like the United Nations.

Obama's remarks on UK remaining in EU get hostile Eurosceptic reaction

24 Jul 2015 11:58

Mr Obama is desperate for our help.

If we can ride into Washington with Liberty we will always come from the high moral ground.

Will Ian Bell view No3 as England's badge of honour ... or with trepidation?

25 Jul 2015 10:10

When I played at Edgbaston I didn't get past 10 so it maybe overly cavalier to offer an opinion, but if Ian can dust off his old Tweed cap, throw away those seeds of doubt, he can let his talent and skill flourish and grow.

This slur on my opinion of the Labour leadership is wrong on every level

25 Jul 2015 09:43

I don't trust Cooper's Balls.

25 Jul 2015 08:53

Blair's Falconer has done enough damage to last a lifetime.

He should pipe down and get back in his red basket.

Speculative Bid declared both a runner and non-runner in Ascot farce

26 Jul 2015 15:27

Regretfully he reverted to type with a bum steer.

'Quarterly capitalism' is short-term, myopic, greedy and dysfunctional

26 Jul 2015 11:10

Fiat money with no cost (zero interest rates) has created these distortions to protect the asset prices which the pyramid is built.

The 40 year experiment of wholly unsound money is being exposed, just like the arrogance of Boris Johnson.

UK growth accelerates; Greece begins talks with creditors - as it happened

28 Jul 2015 09:14

In response to nativeenglishwriter

Dear boy, drugs and prostitution are highly valued by the Treasury and make a significant contribution to the UK's GDP figure, comprende?

28 Jul 2015 08:58

He maybe a spiv but Lord Sewell was only trying to add his contribution to GDP, the Treasury have him under the thumb.

He added 0.0000000033% to GDP, with hindsight I bet he didn't enjoy it.

You can trick yourself into being happy ... if you make life worse first

28 Jul 2015 11:17

Mr Burkeman makes the case for the Morning Star reader quite effectively, but those who like to delve a little deeper into their experience may start to understand that "money without limit causes problems without solution".

Fiat money is a funnel to the elites and the root of all the world's problems.

Google Glass is back! But now it's for businesses?

I want to move science towards art but Google want to move science away from art.

For me, Google is like debt, a dead weight carried around your neck, a yoke which drags everybody down.

The information being collected by the deviant algorithm is so vast and detailed it will eventually be used against us. Any reasoned conclusion must therefore contain resistance.

Google, like all monopolies, is a vermin which needs controlling.

Ed Balls reveals disagreements with Ed Miliband before election

1 Aug 2015 11:15

I think Modesty should be included in Mrs May's list of British Values.

A Brit should try and hide his or hers genius not confirm to everybody that it doesn't exist.

Modesty is like a good photographer, very rare.

Iain Green on the athletics doping allegations – cartoon

3 Aug 2015 10:25

Doping is like human robotics, something I'm sure the MP for Google and mid-Worcestershire would endorse.

The whole world is doping on the fiat US$. Only sound money can clean up this mess.

Economist defends 'Corbynomics' after Chris Leslie's criticism

4 Aug 2015 08:55

In response to John Goodman

you might like to read this : http://www.amazon.co.uk/Propaganda-21st-Century-Power-Ideas/dp/1514621096

4 Aug 2015 08:37

In response to SteveRP

I think you need to brush up on the game of "paper, scissors, stone".

Your scissors aren't sharp enough.

3 Aug 2015 18:22

In response to lechapeaurouge

We are currently moving towards sounder money within the framework of fiat economics run by the Fed. This idea is diametrically opposed to that.

3 Aug 2015 18:02

This is a pre-shambles of an idea and fundamentally unsound.

Nick Symmonds' battle with Nike's corporate autocrats deserves support

Growing student debt is entrenching unfairness for a whole generation

9 Aug 2015 11:33

Mr Hutton has adroitly identified a major trend. If you can't see the major trends then you have no chance of seeing the future.

Under the current proposition of fiat $ economics, every step we take, every tick tock leads us further down the dark path towards a declining number of asset holders and a growing sub-class of individuals swamped by debt, living hand to mouth as opportunities decline and inequality increases.

Saintbury Church on the Worcestershire/Gloucestershire border is a thing of beauty. The other day I was inspecting its spire and came to the conclusion that if highest thoughts transcend, does the spire keep them in or transmit them. I wish the C of E could enlighten its flock?

I still believe a back to basics rebalancing is required, to reform fiat into a hybrid gold standard, making the debt itself valuable by limiting it, like a commodity, by creating a finite supply. Only then can markets be set free from monopolies and unsound money to achieve full productive efficiency. Love without limit, money within limit, is the only way to live in nature, and as everyone can see, nature abhors extremes and always reverts to balance.

Liz Kendall profile: 'I don't want to protest. I want to get into power'

10 Aug 2015 11:30

Liz Kendall is the antithesis of the stage managed show pony. Left to her own devices she would misjudge the weather day in day out, but unfortunately for everyone she is run by Blair's war mongering mouthpiece Portland Communications.

What really shivers her timbers is POWER. In government and politicians, like every heart, bad judgement grows until it's confronted with good arguments which ride in on waves of gilts from the market of public opinion.

Anybody with such an obsession is fundamentally unsound and not worthy of a position to spray around the misguided ideology of her trainer, Blair. Voting for her is voting for big business and would be a retrograde step in the march of time. Sadly, I worry the same applies to at least two of the other candidates.

12 Aug 2015 12:31

Top class journalism.

Yvette Cooper profile: 'You don't have to choose between head and heart'

13 Aug 2015 09:52

The fabien pigeon loft is empty.

Blair's offspring are using obsolete intellectual equipment.

Greg Rutherford blasts 'ridiculous' British kit for world championships

14 Aug 2015 09:33

While under the thrall of the Paper Eagle, we must put up with America's petty jealousies. They can't bare looking at what they really want, to be British, with the Union flag.

We don't need the union jack on Team GB's kit – it's ugly and divisive

14 Aug 2015 16:13

In the spirit of cooperation change the croupier, Mr Jones is dealing crooked cards.

Sundar Pichai: Google's rising star reaches the top (like his teacher said he would)

15 Aug 2015 09:00

I feel the need to wash my hands after reading this nonsense about the deviant algorithm.

Housing is the nation's most urgent and complex challenge. Yet we're paralysed

16 Aug 2015 10:49

Building a fortune is a double-edged sword.

When you can get over that there is more to life than money, an enlightened view is but a stones throw away.

Andy Burnham would allow Labour candidates to stand in Northern Ireland

18 Aug 2015 08:57

"The Papers" on BBC News has to be the best show on television, you get such a good view of the news.

Last night, Goldman's shrill was on rare form. Ms Cooper's cackling was most illuminating; she stirred the pot of bad news with vigour before revealing that only drugs and a photocopier is left in the vaults. Bravo to the BBC News.

Awe: the powerful emotion with strange and beautiful effects

18 Aug 2015 11:01

Mr Burkeman needs to do a lot more thinking.

Awe in nature is known as beauty.

Awe in society is ugly and pernicious.

If he understood the process of money creation, banking and fiat economics, he would see some real shock and awe.

Sebastian Coe can conquer cynicism again but misplaced war analogies must go

20 Aug 2015 08:30

All this doping is a sorry affair.

At dark times like these we should look to our leaders for solace. If the Americans and the Chinese can't keep it clean what hope do the rest of us have?

Blackadder new series on the cards, says Tony Robinson

24 Aug 2015 11:10

If the BBC can remember that the Blackadder flows into the Whiteadder and both end up in BUT, it could be dun to perfection.

One Direction 'to go separate ways in March' following 5th album

24 Aug 2015 08:14

Rumours abound that Louis Tomlinson is to be the new BBC Economics Correspondent, and Harry Styles is to be the Culture Editor at The Spectator.

'A disgrace': BBC condemned by Alex Salmond for referendum coverage

24 Aug 2015 09:25

Alex Salmond has the air of a Blackpool croupier who has mastered the "disappearing chips" routine.

If you ever meet Alex, check you still have a watch and wallet afterwards.

US markets down at closing bell after midday rally as China woes continue – as it happened

25 Aug 2015 08:12

Over the last few days the Chinese and now the Americans have proved concisely that the markets are neither Free or Fair, Capitalistic or Democratic; the State is intervening at every negative juncture. Its Authoritarian and almost Orwellian in nature.

Free market economics is dead in the water.

This leadership race is bigger than Labour: if Corbyn wins, Britain could be out of Europe

25 Aug 2015 09:09

I can smell that one from here.

Can somebody please open the windows of the Guardian office.

Ministers want BBC to consider 'assisted suicide', says Armando Iannucci

27 Aug 2015 10:44

Please forward all comments and suggestions to alan.yentob@hsbbc.co.uk

c/o rona.faircop@hsbbc.co.uk

27 Aug 2015 09:45

What a racket, the BBC is thin gruel at best, the epitome of societal regression at worst.

The news is typified by the revolving door of sheep dipped zombie "journalists" dribbling out inane platitudes, avoiding new or original thought at all cost.

What a state of affairs, I'm just waiting for a new presenter named Dollar Dangerfield to be wheeled out.

What Apple needs to get right with its new iPhone 6S and 6S Plus

29 Aug 2015 10:05

Re Apple's iphone:

Be under no illusions, the camera phone is the modern day mirror, where the vain and deranged drink at the well of Narcissus.

Steven Moffat: 'Only the BBC would have come up with Doctor Who'

29 Aug 2015 08:28

Toot toot, the Gravy Train is here. The BBC love a monopoly and is entirely typical of the wider malaise.

29 Aug 2015 08:22

Listen up Mr Moffatt, people wont suck a sweet you've just picked up from the gutter.

We only have to see an Old Etonian and we salute

3 Oct 2015 12:47

In response to soundofthesuburbs

Because of fiat economics. Fiat money is nothing but paper (debt) with a confidence game attached. As a result you need the slickest salesmen to its bidding and they used to say "When in doubt let the man from Eton do the talking".

The problem is that fiat money only benefits the minority in society at the expensive of the majority, just look the UK Housing market which falling into fewer and fewer hands.

Ultimately the country is held ransom by America's paper eagle and nobody in positions of influence have the gumption or desire to speak up, either a state of denial or cowardice or both.

Markets all around the world are massively overvalued and need to be corrected, the nature of the beast.

3 Oct 2015 10:57

In response to jessthecrip

The mainstream discourse in British politics is currently a faux debate about how solve a housing and inequality time bomb but without letting on that property prices must fall.

3 Oct 2015 10:22

In response to kisunssi

I've had the dubious pleasure of working with the man, which makes me highly informed yet possibly prejudiced.

3 Oct 2015 09:55

Be under no illusions, apart from some exceptional circumstances, a person's life chances are determined prior to birth, so to use Zac Goldsmith's education as a slant on his suitability is naïve.

As far as I'm aware, he had no choice in that matter of his birth and the decisions of his guardians. How he has used his privilege should be the defining feature together with how he has negotiated his gilded path through the lonely desert that is the human experience.

To my mind, the reality of the mayoral campaign will be framed as a choice between a protector of the Judeo Christian traditions of the UK and someone with dubious motives to promote sharia law and to ban interest on money which, in a stroke, would destroy the City.

For the Labour candidate to want to live under sharia subverts the established law of the land is an affront to the rules of decent society. Despite interest rates being basically zero, a desire to turn full circle and implement a backwards and regressive economic ideology should be resisted at all cost.

As a result this makes the Conservative a clear favourite for the job.

Stuart Lancaster's men must climb personal Everests against Australia

3 Oct 2015 11:25

The last game was as farcical as watching Andrew Neil fingering his ring on the BBC's Daily Politics. He must be regretting his decision to forgo a pre-nup. Let's be clear, his bride got married to his collection of modern money. What a dilemma!

In the same vein, England must forget last week. For me, rugby is the perfect game for grading the intelligent animal.

If England can remember the opposition are ruthless creatures, treat them accordingly with disciplined aggression, they can win the day.

ITV is no place for the restless Robert Peston to end up

4 Oct 2015 09:22

As a professional propagandist for fiat economics and the banking interests, everything will seem downhill for Mr Peston after being at the tip of the pyramid otherwise known as the BBC.

Where dreams come true: a fantasia on the theme of a liberal pope

4 Oct 2015 11:22

Unsurprisingly Mr Lee failed to recognise the witty thinly veiled slur on the recent American tour.

The Pope's vehicle of choice: the Fiat, did not go unnoticed in the US corridors of power.

Despite the Vatican's own financial problems, Francis correctly high ticked the issue du jour, which is the financial enslavement of the world under the low flying Paper Eagle, corrupting all aspects of life with increasing volumes of bad, unsound paper money backed by nothing but a empty promise at the barrel of a gun.

Maybe Mrs Yellen told him more QE is on the way.

In need of a perfect conference speech, David Cameron? Here's the recipe

5 Oct 2015 13:30

I have to say David Cameron is an insufferable specimen, the type who counts his blessings for the all the poor and uninformed that he can exploit.

His useful life must be nearly over, he should slither aside and let Mr Osborne get on with the job.

Theresa May announces drive to limit right to claim asylum in UK

6 Oct 2015 14:15

The leadership contest must be in full swing, apparently Mrs May's bag carriers are going round the conference telling anyone who will listen

"they call him Gideon because he's been on more hotel beds than the Bible"

IMF warns of stagnation threat to G7 economies

8 Oct 2015 11:35

In response to TokyoJones

When trading a so called "normal market" I agree sell high / buy low but I get the impression you are talking from the position of government. Governments have a very bad track record in repaying their debt, it is generally rolled building a bigger pile. If you believe that the monetary system will "recover" you must be assuming that interest rates will rise again. If this is the case, government debt will be rolled at higher rates making its servicing unsustainable with debt/GDP approaching 100%.

Conversely, when you look again at the US, it is no coincidence that their 30+year bull market in Govt bonds coincides with the implementation of fully fledged fiat. Considering fiat has no intrinsic value its unsurprising that its interest rate (or the cost of money) has reverted to zero.

The result is that the fiat monetary system is trapped even though statistics are being gamed to the point of farce. Despite rampant asset price inflation, they cant raise rates otherwise they put housing and stocks into a bear market. To maintain the status quo they can only engage in more stimulus aka "printing" and/or send nominal rates negative. All this does is kick the problem down the road and infact make the problem even worse as inequality grows and productivity falls. It all represents a continued crisis in confidence with a currency predicated on confidence. When this is mirrored onto human economic behaviour the confusion and lack of confidence manifests itself in stagnation. Collectively society has lost faith in its money and the institutions managing it.

In my opinion, and in the absence of a new genuine commodity currency they can either unleash these managed markets to self correct and see who is swimming naked or alternatively continue playing with the concept of a synthetic commodity currency using the government debt itself in the form of a debt ceiling. I worry, in the US especially, that due to a lack of leadership and deeply entrenched vested interests, we have reached a collective inertia which only an unexpected and violent financial or physical event will breach.

7 Oct 2015 11:11

In response to TokyoJones

Money is a complex subject formed from simple principles. Using the US as the example, In 100 years the dollar it has crumbled from a pure gold standard to a gold standard with fractional reserve to a fully unhinged fiat currency.

The price or value of anything, including a currency, is determined by supply and demand. Under a gold standard or commodity money, its value is determined by a finite supply and the hard work needed to retrieve it. Fiat money has no value other than that given to it by a governments law and the process of creating it.

Fiat money is actually just debt. When you borrow from the bank, the money is created out of thin air to loan to you. The supply of fiat money is formed by the issuance of debt. The process of debt itself can be understood as simply spending the future today. In other words, debt is borrowing wealth from the future or effectively from the next generation. (The real life example is getting your children to pay $500k for a house that would have cost you $50k)

When this process is understood you can see the value of fiat currency is an illusion maintained by a game of confidence between the issuer (banks) and the general public (the borrower).

Banks create illusions of wealth as asset prices are forced higher by the issuance of more debt (fiat money). If borrowers all paid back their loans, asset prices would collapse, therefore you can see banks create pyramid schemes of wealth based on money which costs them nothing to create on which interest is charged.

The issuers of the currency control the fortunes of the people but this fact is never advertised which makes banking and money lending with fiat money one shrouded in deceit.

The result of this process of obfuscation permeates throughout society whereby all business is based on varying degrees of deception (for example VW emissions etc etc).

So ultimately, the choice of currency type comes down to one of morality. Money which is limited is honest and good, whereas fiat money is inherently dishonest and bad.

Where do you stand?

6 Oct 2015 18:46

Another article without a mention of monetary theory and why it's of fundamental importance.

Money is the thing encapsulates all our values because we value all our wants and desires in it. In fact to talk about anything else in life is really just hot air and bluster.

Everything has a value which makes "the money" so powerful it is the most important thing in most people's lives. The current problems stem from the fact the current monetary system is based on a classic pyramid Ponzi scheme of debt which has been exposed and confidence in it has been deeply undermined. Fiat (or paper) money is a pyramid scheme because its continued value and existence requires the issuance of layers upon layers of new debt. It is like a Ponzi scheme because it is sold as something it is not. It is sold as safe and secure, yet it is maintained by a game of confidence played between the politian's / bankers and the general public.

More and more people, businesses and organisation are now working this out and the result is an increasing lack of confidence and a desire for the old principles of sound money. As Glencore has recently shown this desire makes current asset prices highly over-valued.

SABMiller agrees AB Inbev takeover deal of £68bn

13 Oct 2015 10:14

In response to optimist99

Thanks for that, I promise I wont hold a grievance over your ignorance.

13 Oct 2015 08:44

In response to quinlanmicheal

Agreed, boycotts are the only thing these people understand and take seriously.

Like in all disputes and grievances its sometimes best to think, not what x or y has done to you, rather what you can still do to x or y.

13 Oct 2015 08:18

Proof entirely that globalisation is pro corporate monopolies and negative for all consumers.

Half of world's wealth now in hands of 1% of population – report

14 Oct 2015 10:07

On the day of this illuminating report, listening to the Today programme on Radio 4 isolated the problem that society faces perfectly. In all discussion regarding budgets or finance the ideological position of the organisation is to conflate debt with wealth, talking about debt as an asset. The fact is that only banks call debt an asset.

Everything they do is predicated on the deception, yes deception, that debt is wealth and therefore debt is good. Debt is wealth and good for banks but for everybody else it is a liability to be managed. This makes the BBC a dangerous and wholly prejudiced organisation. In this case, it was Justin Webb doing the deceiving and remember con men and women the world over are, by definition, some of the most plausible characters your likely to meet.

By why highlight the BBC? The answer is simple, the likes of Sky, for example, don't purport to be independent, its raison d'etre is to make money at all cost, the BBC purports to be independent and impartial, something which is obviously untrue. Unless they change the tune on this crucial, omnipresent issue their reputation can only be further tarnished and one of a propagandist for the banks.

'Living within our means' makes no economic sense. Labour is right to oppose it

14 Oct 2015 20:10

In response to Doooot

You have to remember we, as a country, do not operate in isolation. Whilst continuing along this road of fiat economics we are beholden to a competitive confidence game, held ransom by the highest bidder, which is currently the US$, operated by the Federal Reserve. Each country is playing a confidence game with its money relative to each others. This is the guillotine, the cleverest trick of all. If we, as you and the labour party suggest, print money via the BofE to directly finance the consumption of the general public, we would signal loud and clear to the rest of the world, our trading partners and creditors, that the money we use is fundamentally unsound, simply pieces of paper backed by nothing but a state of affairs. Markets would sell the pound and bring the whole UK economy into disarray. Considering the UK has a large trade deficit, you can see how the spiral of negatives would start. Believe me, financial markets are vicious and rapacious beasts when blood is in the water. You could do well to read some more at www.zanadome.com

14 Oct 2015 17:44

In response to Doooot

I'm afraid you are ill informed. The guy is dangerous because he wants to continue, with vigour, the broken and flawed system of fiat economics, the same confidence game which has enslaved you and your children in debt, ensuring future generations will be poorer than you, in rented accommodation while a minority suck on the money funnel of a pyramid scheme. Money without limit creates problems without solution, I suggest you try and get your head around some of these issues.

14 Oct 2015 11:49

Ha-joon Chang is an extremely dangerous man.

Britain has made 'visionary' choice to become China's best friend, says Xi

18 Oct 2015 09:15

We face a stark choice, do we want to be beholden to the dodgy $, the paper eagle, or do we want to have a look at the Confucius loving Yuan?

Supposedly, Confucius believed "never do to anybody what you wouldn't want done to yourself". That may be all well and good, but when the other side is swinging through the trees, lying, robbing and cheating you've got to change your attitude.

To my mind, the Americans have had a good go at world domination and have failed on every level. The playing field needs to be levelled so we can make our economics and money sound again.

Big Magic: Creative Living Beyond Fear by Elizabeth Gilbert review – lessons in life from the Eat, Pray, Love author

23 Oct 2015 09:09

I'm a big fan of Zoe Williams, she is clearly the best writer on the Guardian which is why I must write this plea here.

Reading the Guardian today you would be led to think everything is swell, yet yesterday, in the real world, the financial world which controls our fortunes, they were running rampant over the future.

In Europe the ECB's Mario Draghi has gone full psycho and is priming the markets for negative nominal rates and more QE. For the uninitiated this means him printing more funny money with which to buy stocks and his employers bonds and pushing euro interest rates below zero whereby euro-citizens will be charged interest on having a positive balance in their accounts. The money is so worthless, it costs you to keep it - thereby forcing you to consider spending it. Saving is dead in this mad, bad, new world.

Over the pond, the US Govt is about to raise its Debt ceiling again to over 19 trillion $, admits cries from the politian's that living without borrowing is suicidal. Let's be clear, the US isn't borrowing from the rest of the world, it is borrowing from itself, the Federal Reserve, and it has no intention of ever paying it back. If that doesn't sound perverse and dangerous I don't know what does.

Add on top, the fact that there is not a peep about this systematically important news from the BBC and other mainstream media, you can only conclude that a qualified deception is being conducted on the unsuspecting public. To prove me wrong, I challenge Zoe Williams (and the Guardian), to grab her lady bollocks and enlighten the public to this unprecedented monetary experiment before the problem gets so out of hand that people are forced onto the streets to stop it.

England's churches can survive – but the religion will have to go

22 Oct 2015 10:07

In the battle between good and evil, or as an economist would say, between sound and unsound money, the prevailing winds are undoubtedly bad.

The thing with evil is that it prays on the weakness of the human condition, in particular the propensity to suffer from denial. To look, unblinkered at the state of the world, you can clearly see the daily dose of financial news is one of corruption and downright fraud at the heart of major companies and institutions. It's as though fraud and corruption is now endemic. Add to that, financial markets which view bad news as good, and good news as bad, you can see the established order of things is the residence of evil.

Why is it that journalists and commentators, those who hold the keys to public opinion, remain so unexercised by this climate of endemic corruption? Is it because they are ignorant about the power of "the money" or have they become corrupted themselves and suffer from the weakness that is a state of denial? While the CofE remain mute, unfortunately I suspect it's the latter.

China interest rate cut fuels fears over ailing economy

25 Oct 2015 09:15

The PBOC are signalling to the market that the reality on the ground is far worse than previously thought. To surprise a market when their stocks are at recent highs is incongruent with rationality.

The direction of travel towards negative nominal rates in a paper system is an admittance that this fantasy experiment with unsound money is over and the end of the yellow brick road is in sight.

English wine pioneers rush to start UK vineyards

26 Oct 2015 08:24

This is a highly misleading and/or uninformed article.

With the price of agricultural land at record highs it is now uneconomic to enter any traditional agri-business. This increase in numbers will represent existing landowners diversifying into a highly questionable venture. In wine making the terroir is everything and in this area the UK isn't blessed. As a simple comparison, how will UK producers compete with, say the French, when land in costs 1/10th of the UK (£1k+ acre vs £10k+ acre in UK).

The bottom line is that the UK has shackled itself to the banks and the money funnel. Only a re-alignment of property values can save the UK now.

Britain is heading for another 2008 crash: here's why

28 Oct 2015 12:04

This is a very naïve positive critique of fiat money and completely ignores the fact that this unsound money has only been in operation for some 40 years. It also ignores the fact that every fiat currency in history, bar none, has ended in failure and collapse.

Apocalypse now: has the next giant financial crash already begun?

2 Nov 2015 09:33

Could Mr Mason please stop using Keynes as some paragon of truth because he was operating in an age which started to dismantle the gold standard with fractional reserve banking and consequently bares no resemblance to the currency of today . With today's fiat money, the link with time is that you are bringing consumption forward from the future, effectively spending your children's fortunes today.

The surveillance bill is as big a threat to state security as to individual liberty

5 Nov 2015 09:57

If power corrupts completely, the "all-seeing eye" needs a patch not bifocals. Surely people can see which way the weather is blowing or is the "conditioning" stronger than I suspected?

5 Nov 2015 09:24

Only those who support the dystopian future of the omnipotent State that is protecting the sandcastle of fiat money will support this bill.

Bank of England: governor Carney has 'no regrets' after leaving rates unchanged again - live

5 Nov 2015 11:22

In response to Spike501

Rent and Mortgage payments make up 50%+ of the average income; the food industry has hidden inflation with smaller packaging; energy, council tax, entertainment etc all in a positive trend - in short, the cost of living is undoubtedly rising.

Unless the froth is taken out of the financial and financialised markets (housing) we are heading to negative nominal rates which will destroy the system from the inside. Being paid to borrow, or charged to deposit and save signals the system is surrounded by a minefield. The idea is perverse and incongruent with accepted and rational thought. If fiat money is based on debt and the price of debt isn't positive, the value of money is being negative and therefore being destroyed which means private investment dries up, economic activity slows, only black markets will grow. Money has to have a positive value otherwise acuminating it has no benefit; the ultimate result is that the only economic incentive would be to earn enough to cover everyday expenses. To maintain the current system central bankers have to unshackle the markets and let them find their own levels, like they should have done in 2008. The process of extend and pretend since Lehman has to come to an end.

5 Nov 2015 08:44

Please, please, please remember that inflation data is purposely manipulated lower by excluding the largest element of personal expenditure, rent or mortgage payments from the basket of prices. (real-life inflation is running at between 3-5%+). Mr Carney will tear away the remaining thread of creditability if he uses "inflation data" as an argument for not raising rates. The prospect of negative nominal rates means Capitalism itself demands rates must rise.

Many non-religious people still believe in God – what is that all about?

9 Nov 2015 19:08

Although I wouldn't dare be as bold as to dismiss the likelihood of unknown unknowns, I must humbly evacuate a personal understanding that God exists on earth, in fact there are many Gods, and they come in the form of anything you have invested your emotions in. Invested emotions are also known as vested interests.

It could be a Church, a football team, a relationship, a company share price, a pet, an antique, a special recipe, the list is potentially endless. When interests are vested they hold a power over you. When you become emotionally beholden, that entity has powers to determine your future, you believe in them and thus your emotions have been captured; they can act and you follow, like a master and servant.

Your vested interests and emotions play the part of Gods

If the truth be known, the omnipotent God on this earth is the US Federal Reserve. They control the dollar and the tax on time (inflation).

In the game about fiat money: "Paper, Scissors, Stone", the "paper" is represented by the $, the "stone" by the US military, and the "scissors" by the cutting argument. The Fed don't have the scissors, they can be found in places such as http://www.zanadome.com

Athletics Australia backs calls to ban Russia from Olympics after Wada report

10 Nov 2015 11:13

In response to truk10

Dick Pound is obviously prejudiced. Coe can't use blinkered ignorance as a plausible defence. He is either complicit, incompetent or both.

Sebastain Coe proves concisely that being good at running around a track, like a talented greyhound, doesn't make you principled or competent in the realm of regulation. Coe obviously excels in hubris and sense of entitlement which makes him entirely typical of the modern day Politian.

It was obvious to anyone who has spent a day in their life in the real world that doping was rife in the sport. Coe was undoubtedly complicit and more interested in protecting his position in the "cosy club of privilege" than clean up his sport. This makes him unsuitable, at every conceivable level, to play any further part in the administration of the sport.

Government puts plans to relax Sunday trading laws on hold – Politics live

10 Nov 2015 13:09

The PM has correctly highlighted that only "chaos" changes the old "order", followed by a new "order" out of the "chaos".

Chaos outs the order, order out of the chaos.

David Cameron signals flexibility on migrant benefits in EU letter

10 Nov 2015 17:55

In response to polwulky

An interesting point but I'd like to point out the PM might not have any support from the BBC. Those frothing quislings are currently repressing legitimate and intelligent pro-European argument in the comments section of their website. For all the people complaining, they must understand that the BBC have no interest in a 2 sided argument, only points of discussion which suit their thinly veiled position.

10 Nov 2015 17:09

In response to isanythingleft

Yes, I understand your point and I'm sympathetic to it but we must take into account human nature and the likely response. In such as situation, for right or wrong, the "jilted" party will hold a legitimate grievance. We must expect a reaction. The response will be one of thinly veiled spite and retribution. They will find any, and all ways to show us the error of our decision.

In essence, some in Brussels, will consider a BREXIT a de facto declaration of war.

10 Nov 2015 14:08

I wish we would get this referendum over and done with. Everybody knows deep down we won't vote to leave because if we left the family of Europe we would be ostracized like a paedophile on a council estate.

The Guardian view on David Cameron's speech on Europe: time to end the phoney war

10 Nov 2015 20:13

In response to AllieClark

I'm just saying the reaction and consequences have to be factored into the calculus of your decision making. Your analogy is somewhat valid only in that the "violent partner" also happens to be the biggest customer of your small business and is also the local magistrate with connections at the highest level.

10 Nov 2015 19:37

I wish we would get this referendum over and done with. Everybody knows deep down we won't vote to leave because if we left the family of Europe we would be ostracized like a paedophile on a council estate.

I am sympathetic to some "leave" arguments but we must take into account human nature and the likely response. In such a situation, for right or wrong, the "jilted" party will hold a legitimate grievance. We must expect a reaction. The response will be one of thinly veiled spite and retribution. They will find any, and all ways to show us the error of our decision.

In essence, some in Brussels, will legitimately consider a BREXIT a de facto declaration of war.

More City reforms needed, Bank of England governor tells forum

11 Nov 2015 11:53

Conducting this charade in a Church is surely plumbing the depths.

Buy-to-let mortgages at highest level since 2007, says CML

11 Nov 2015 17:24

It's about time these blood-sucking vampires feel some pain inflicted by the tightening cycle.

And by the way, not a line in the Guardian about Count Draghi who is about to directly fund city and regional deficits - this is real news. The ECB is in complete denial and is now conjuring with fully unhinged fiat economics.

Islington Community Theatre gives young people a voice – here is why you should listen

12 Nov 2015 10:18

Maybe these young people can find their voice to complain why they will never be able to afford a house and have to pay usury levels of rent to a rampant rentier class for the rest of their lives.

Learning to trust bankers again is the very worst thing we could do

12 Nov 2015 17:27

Heads up Giles, be under no illusions, bankers only do what central bankers and regulators allow them.

Central bankers claim they saved the world by bailing out the failed businesses which of course is utter nonsense. They bailed out their mates and got government, and by extension, the population to pay for it. Please understand, these people are not working for your benefit.

By taking a huge suck on the "funny money funnel" central bankers have ensured your children, and their children, will have to work harder, for longer, for less, and in probably rented accommodation. The truth is that the decisions of these people were cowardly and reprehensible, yet no politician or commentator has the gumption to bring them to account. Unless you are hopelessly naïve you will be able to come to your

Roy Hodgson counts on Ross Barkley to be England's counterattack king

12 Nov 2015 23:09

Re: The Captain: The Manager is making a mistake. He should be planning and forming the side around the most intelligent player; everything good flows around and through Rooney, his form (temporary vs permanent class) is a reflection on the United Manager and therefore should be discounted. I would pick Wayne at 10 every, every, every time.

Northern Rock mortgages are latest gamble for US private equity firm Cerberus

13 Nov 2015 17:22

Good luck to them, but Cerberus should be in full cognizance that if these mortgages go south they won't get bailed out.

A brief history of underwear: V&A exhibition goes big on the smalls

14 Nov 2015 11:34

V&A sink to new lows.

Sun slams Corbyn's nod and gets a rise out of me

15 Nov 2015 08:54

Stewart Lee is funny, with a brilliant turn of phase, I particularly like his library euphemism. On Wednesday morning at 11am he was reportedly seen berating a man on a mobility scooter outside the Hampstead branch of Wetherspoons. A little more decorum is needed please Stewart.

The innovators: the LiquiGlide coating that gets mayonnaise out of the bottle

16 Nov 2015 12:23

Congratulations to the bofins at MIT, you are really helping move humanity along, solving the biggest problems of the day.

After Paris, Europe may never feel as free again

15 Nov 2015 14:41

In response to LansanaDia

Yes, I am British. I agree the Iraq War was a disgrace which I disagreed with then and now. As for the slave trade, it's too long ago to take responsibility for that.

15 Nov 2015 11:33

Of course, these attacks were designed to sow division between "them and us". Inevitably they will succeed in that goal. The French PM has already declared war on the ideology of an Islamic State. If Muslims want to dispel the belief that Islam is the most primitive of religions and incompatible with western society, the followers and acolytes must be seen publically to absolve themselves from the actions perpetrated in Paris. Silence will inevitably be considered complicity.

This is not to isolate one religion, all those who believe in a "man in the sky" actually believe in an irrational figment of their imaginations. They have become beholden to an idea which they have emotionally vested interests in. Believing in "God" is wholly emotional and therefore primitive and unenlightened. If they could master the double truth that "enlightenment is emotionless and emotionless is enlightenment", the ability to see beauty without desire, maybe things would be different.

Those who want to manipulate and control your emotions, play god, are dangerous and should be resisted. For me, these abhorrent attacks just confirm that those who act on behalf of an "other worldly god" are wholly untrustworthy because they are irrational and therefore inherently unpredictable. It is hard to defend the right of such people to believe in such things when it is such patent nonsense and directly impinges on others.

Japan 's 'quintuple dip' recession delivers a fresh blow to Abenomics

16 Nov 2015 12:36

Japan is an intellectual and economic wasteland and the blueprint vision of fiat money. The stock and JGB market dominated on a daily basis by direct Central Bank participation. The idea of free and fair price discovery shattered on the floor of a command and control economy.

Mindless terrorists? The truth about Isis is much worse

16 Nov 2015 12:10

In response to ardvark2

The hypocrisy surrounding Assad is appalling.

16 Nov 2015 10:55

When Donald Trump looks like the least worst option for the future of humanity you've got question the new depths that we are plumbing with unsound fiat money.

16 Nov 2015 10:27

All this senseless violence belies a deeper and more inconvenient truth for individuals and those who govern us. Ignoring the evidence that the savages of Islamic State are using American made and/or supplied weapons, many see this as the final battle of old ideas and beliefs, that of Christianity vs Islam.

It is inconvenient because it doesn't fit with the desire of supra-national entities to create an overarching omnipotent government state whereby financial, followed by human capital, can move freely across the globe, using unsound fiat money and mainstream media propaganda.

The two directions of travel are diametrically opposed which suggests conflict and disharmony is guaranteed. Islam wants to bring the battle to Europe whereas Christianity and Government want to contain the battle in the Middle East. Unless some intelligent decisions are made soon, the open borders of Southern Europe may ensure both areas are battle grounds. The time for action is upon us and some binary options must be put on the table.

Japan enters recession again as Abenomics falters

16 Nov 2015 19:17

Absolutely correct; only hubris, denial and "not on my watch" is holding this pyramid of cards up.

16 Nov 2015 16:37

Japan is an intellectual and economic wasteland and the blueprint vision of fiat money. The stock and JGB market dominated on a daily basis by direct Central Bank participation. The idea of free and fair price discovery shattered on the floor of a command and control economy.

Japan's three arrows of Abenomics continue to miss their targets

17 Nov 2015 09:33

Japan is an intellectual and monetary wasteland and the blueprint vision of fiat money. The stock and JGB market dominated on a daily basis by direct Central Bank participation. The idea of free and fair price discovery shattered on the floor of a command and control economy.

Terror can only succeed with our cooperation

17 Nov 2015 10:00

As in nature, some things, like Christianity and Islam, just don't mix. Extreme multiculturalism is like mixing oil and water. The scientific term is immiscible.

Why can't those in authority finally admit the political and social experiment of extreme multiculturalism is immiscible with national security?

UK inflation remained negative at -0.1% in October

17 Nov 2015 12:02

The insufferable propagandists at the BBC are spinning/claiming that deflation is good because it puts more money in people's pockets. If that were the case why does the BofE have a +2% inflation mandate?

Markets remain nervous on Paris fears - as it happened

18 Nov 2015 08:17

Some friendly advice for Mark Carney - when your in a hole - stop digging.

The sight of a reporter expressing emotion is a sign of the times

18 Nov 2015 18:22

The constructed reality of Anne Perkins is likely to be incorrect. I suspect that the reporter was shedding tears of remorse and regret based on his organisations generational agenda of promoting extreme multiculturalism with immiscible religions.

With solutions so thin on the ground, may I suggest one? Islam is in tatters, it can't even get along with itself. The Shia / Sunni divide is just as deep as Islam / Christianity. As PM Cameron said, we could cut the head off the snake, so to speak, by unilaterally withdrawing from the Middle East. With the money saved, we could finance all supporters of Islam to go over, choose sides and have it out, once and for all. The winner takes the "mountain of black gold" and they can live over there in peace. It would be like running the Crusades in reverse.

With no other solution articulated, this one must be the best. What say you?

Interest rate hikes likely in December, Federal Reserve minutes reveal

18 Nov 2015 23:55

What could possibly go wrong when bad new is good and good news is bad? - the answer can only be that the insane, deranged and programmed are left long stocks now.

UK retail sales fall hints at pre-Christmas lull

19 Nov 2015 12:22

In my opinion, the asset markets are displaying quite preposterous levels of denial.

In the current environment, where staggering amount of debt have been added to the system at historically low rates, the sensitivity of interest rate movements has been increased. A move from 0.25 to 0.75% will now be as restrictive a tightening measure as a historic move from 2 to 4%. The elasticity of rate movements has been dramatically increased. This leaves two scenarios:

1. The reserve currency tightens credit conditions as expected in December. The trajectory for asset prices is lower.

2. To loosen or maintain current conditions, by adding even more debt to an already overloaded system, means, due to the increased elasticity, that the subsequent tightening is brought forward and will be more violent. Asset price can therefore only be maintained on a diminishing basis.

In conclusion, the system is trapped in its own constructed reality and can only be repaired by a re-alignment of asset prices. On the balance of probabilities, current levels can only be maintained if the world stops turning and no further events occur. The only trade with a positive probability of success, on any time horizon, is to sell what you own.

Draghi: ECB ready to act in light of weakest eurozone recovery since 1998 - as it happened

Mr Draghi is asking banks to commit Hari Kari but understandably they are quite sceptical.

Lending to an already indebted economy at historically low rates is a suicidal trade. The bottom line is that the debtor would not be able to survive a normalisation of rates.

Asset markets are at the top of the cycle and banks are behaving accordingly with rational self-interest. As perverse as it sounds, banks would rather pay Germany or even Italy to borrow 2 yr notes than lend to the "real economy" and force a bigger implosion just round the corner.

Should authority figures hide their emotions?

21 Nov 2015 17:48

Personally, I'm more interested in how Cameron wants to railroad the UK into a Syrian bombing campaign. Let's face it, he doesn't have a good track record in decision making. How does he expect to bomb an idea into submission?

It seems to me, with over reactions and likely false flags flying all over the place, the PM is again being disingenuous and the only place to go after the bombing fails is a ground campaign. The arguments (and no plan) being given to parliament and the public are insulting.

Welby bids to defuse Church of England's 'demographic time bomb'

21 Nov 2015 23:13

The CofE has descended to being just an evangelical hedge fund for fiat economics.

UK could join Syria airstrikes before Christmas, Osborne suggests

22 Nov 2015 11:48

Mr Cameron may think he was born to lead but he won't be leading me, like a lemming, over his cliff of extreme and unworkable ideas. The waters of his invisible plan are so clouded I wouldn't be surprised if it transpires that Vitol is the trader behind the ISIS oil.

Why the Sun's 'jihadi' poll is dubious — and its headline dangerous

I'm sure "1 in 5" is a gross under-estimation, after all they are only following written instructions.

That said, this latest drum beat to war by the PM is still another foreign miscalculation. His war cries are now being joined by military leaders. Don't forget these good men, trained to fight and kill, understandably get gun-ho at the prospect of the fight but it doesn't excuse the lives and treasure which will be wasted, just so the PM can say he's got balls around the banquet table.

This problem is one of idea's between the Sunni and Shia and they should be allowed to have it out in peace.

The Guardian view on the BBC: a contract with the people, not the government

24 Nov 2015 12:17

In the City, it is an accepted truism there are 2 types of people in this world; those who are working for the banks and those who are working for sound commodity money. Which one are you?

Allow me to explain with factual truth. The job of central bankers and their gatekeepers of accepted truth, in the BBC, academia and the media, is to make the simple principles of fiat money complicated.

Under commodity money, such as the gold standard, the amount of money was limited by nature and hard work. Under fiat money, the amount of money has been given over to the banks to increase at will by the issuance of debt in the form of loans.

In 2008, the banks were bankrupt and blew up the economy by creating an unsustainable bubble in the UK property market. We have been repaying their losses ever since. The correct response should have been to allow the banks to fail and the Government to reintroduce commodity money to prevent a repeat. Until they do, boom, bust, crisis, rising inequality and moral decline will continue as your children are plunged further and further into un-repayable debt.

Awake from your slumber of ignorance and have yourself a thought experiment and reach the enlightened conclusion that unless you're changing the mind of government back to commodity money, every minute of your life is spent working for the banks.

Mark Carney testifies to parliament; US growth revised up - as it happened

To prove they weren't picked for their lack of intelligence, will the Select Committee ask Mr Carney at least one adult question:

Negative nominal rates have been announced for individual account holders at an EU bank. Will you resign if they occur in the UK?

Consumer spending rise troubles Bank of England

24 Nov 2015 19:35

When he talks about "helicopter money" he opens Pandora's box - the idea is incongruous with the concept of austerity. The layman immediately thinks "when he can print money out of thin air for free, why is the government cutting my benefit's or departmental budget?"

24 Nov 2015 18:33

In response to kimdriver

Yes I did and he has no comprehension or solution to the harm he is causing.

24 Nov 2015 16:08

Andy Haldane was thrashing around in the Select committee lido clearly out of his depth.

Cameron is letting oil-rich Gulf bullies dictate his foreign policy

25 Nov 2015 09:08

What does Cameron think he's doing? He is taking Parliament and the British people for fools as he defends abhorrent regimes like Turkey and Saudi who both, according to mainstream reports, are supporting ISIS, trading their fuel, funding and protecting them. What difference will sending a handful of old jets make?

Thankfully, Parliament and MP's still have a chance to save Cameron from himself.

Spending review 2015: George Osborne scraps tax credit cuts and freezes police budget - as it happened

25 Nov 2015 12:13

In response to ukchange68

that or he would have to do another forfeit with a broom, black suspenders and Golden Labrador.

25 Nov 2015 11:57

I'm most looking forward to the contemptible arrogance and hubris of Andrew Neil talking nonsense after the event without mentioning the words: fiat economics, negative real rates, money funnel or Ponzi scheme.

How can the viewer rationally believe the BBC has their best interests at heart when they promote and legitimise a financial system which is based on unlimited money and debt, borrowing from the next generation but concealing and supressing the fact from them?

What else can a confidence game, a deception waged against your children, be called?

When you can't be honest about the money, everything else you subsequently do is a fraud. I'm sure his new wife would concur.

The science of swing: a pink ball's journey from tannery to Adelaide Oval

25 Nov 2015 22:13

In response to recliner

I'm saying nothing derogatory towards women, this is about the attack on heterosexual masculinity.

25 Nov 2015 14:57

Be under no illusions, the feminisation of professional sport is under way. The propagandists and central planners, at organisations like the BBC, are trying to break the back of masculinity in sport as well as everyday life.

The introduction of imagery designed to psychologically conflict with traditional values is an orchestrated attack. It is designed to break the will and image of the strong heterosexual man in traditional roles. What better place trial it in the game of cricket than in Australia.

In my opinion, this brand of deviance, and the minions such as this author who do the bidding, should be resisted in order to preserve the natural values and history from which sport is derived.

It's time either to clean up sport or put the Teletubbies in charge

25 Nov 2015 18:12

The corruption, moral and financial, has seeped into every orifice of society and all because of the unsound fiat dollar and the Federal Reserve. This is now undisputable, proven by the fact that the establishment, including the the BBC, supress even the discussion of the issue. It's like denying the weather forecast or football results exist - statements of fact which are important to know and understand.

The Guardian needs change this ASAP before they vote "Hilary Clinton's brain in a fish tank" into the white house.

Cameron sets out 'moral case' for airstrikes against Isis in Syria – Politics live

26 Nov 2015 11:56

You can feel the madness and bloodlust building, an unwinnable religious war against multiple unknown enemies in multiple unknown locations at any and all cost. Cameron and these people are not for stopping now. The Commons had better vote for war otherwise I worry the British people should expect some dark events proving that MP's voted the wrong way.

<Aside: it's reported in multiple locations that Erdogan's son is the conduit trading ISIS oil into the West>

Britain, France needs you in this fight against Isis

26 Nov 2015 18:55

The strongest argument I've heard so far for airstrikes on Syria is that our sophisticated missiles are more accurate when fired by us rather than the Saudi's. What does that say for the rest of the PM's pleading?

Labour leadership at odds over Syrian airstrikes

27 Nov 2015 10:00

As all governments, both light and dark, know - never let a crisis go to waste. Jeremy Corbyn is being handed the perfect opportunity to remove the thorn in his party's side - the Blairites.

It is now time to trade the situation well and use the "march to war vote" as a golden opportunity to remove the yoke which is dragging him and this Labour Party backwards. The MP's in question have no interest in doing the right thing, they are playing a darker, more sinister game on behalf of wider forces. He was selected as leader for his views and at times of "crisis" he must command loyalty within the party.

Hilary Benn tells Corbyn: I'm doing my job in supporting Syria airstrikes

27 Nov 2015 18:45

Politics is done by human beings, human beings are intelligent animals (even you darling), and animals are part of nature.

In response to ATII

Politics is like nature - constantly trying to achieve balance. Extremes are met by extremes, balance is met by balance. Action and re-action, counter-balance is the nature of politics.

In response to Elinore

I hope your kids like paying debt interest.

If I were you I'd worry about the here and now because the debt built by your Blair and Brown means the future has already been spent.

27 Nov 2015 10:42

As all governments, both light and dark, know - never let a crisis go to waste. Jeremy Corbyn is being handed the perfect opportunity to remove the thorn in his party's side - the Blairites.

It is now time to trade the situation well and use the "march to war vote" as a golden opportunity to remove the yoke which is dragging him and this Labour Party backwards. The MP's in question have no interest in doing the right thing, they are playing a darker, more sinister game on behalf of wider forces. He was selected as leader for his views and at times of "crisis" he must command loyalty within the party - Take the lead and whip the Vote.

Sun article on Coronation Street 'jihadi' plot denied by ITV

27 Nov 2015 20:25

If MP's vote for war they will have to ban the burqa at the same time. As the Swiss have just pronounced, it would be a national security risk.

The first casualty of war debate is uncertainty

27 Nov 2015 18:35

Don't forget the PM's most famous and favourite phase: "Look, I won't lie to you, well that was one, but I promise not to do it again".

That might be very clever but lying about war is something else and his are piling up like dead bodies:
1. there are 70,000 moderate chaps ready to do our bidding;
2. we are in mortal national danger from this unsuccessful and invisible threat ;
3. we've got loads of spare cash we can spend on missiles costing £1m a pop.;
4. The Saudi's aren't financing ISIS
5. The son of Turkey's Erdogan isn't the trader behind the ISIS oil shall I go on?

Labour's rift over Syria risks turning into a battle for the party's soul

28 Nov 2015 17:55

Update from yesterday

Don't forget the PM's most famous and favourite phase: "Look, I won't lie to you, well that was one, but I promise not to do it again".

That might be very clever but lying about war is something else and his are piling up like dead bodies:
1. there are 70,000 moderate chaps ready to do our bidding;
2. we are in mortal national danger from this unsuccessful and

invisible threat ;

3.we've got loads of spare cash we can spend on missiles costing £1m a pop.;

4. The Saudi's aren't financing ISIS

5. The son of Turkey's Erdogan isn't the trader behind the ISIS oil

Daily update:

6. We need to support Turkey which doesn't assassinate prominent lawyers

7. We need to support the US which hasn't been supplying weapons to the other side for years

8. We don't need a diversion from the start of the economic tightening cycle

9. Turkish supported jihadist group isn't shelling Russian base in Syria

10. This war won't be used as cover to take away more civil liberties at home

Jeremy Corbyn warns rebels: I'm not going anywhere over Syria

29 Nov 2015 12:00

Don't forget the PM's most famous and favourite phase: "Look, I won't lie to you, well that was one, but I promise not to do it again".

That might be very clever but lying about war is something else and his are piling up like dead bodies:

1. there are 70,000 moderate chaps ready to do our bidding;

2. we are in mortal national danger from this unsuccessful and invisible threat ;

3.we've got loads of spare cash we can spend on missiles costing £1m a pop.;

4. The Saudi's aren't financing ISIS
5. The son of Turkey's Erdogan isn't the trader behind the ISIS oil

Daily update:

6. We need to support Turkey which doesn't assassinate prominent lawyers
7. We need to support the US which hasn't been supplying weapons to the other side for years
8. We don't need a diversion from the start of the economic tightening cycle
9. Turkish supported jihadist group isn't shelling Russian base in Syria
10. This war won't be used as cover to take away more civil liberties at home

Daily Update and coup de grace

11. We may have lost the arguments but we are absolutely not going to war just for me to save face

World leaders call for action at Paris climate talks – as it happened

30 Nov 2015 11:33

Prince Charles is absolutely right, "your today should not trump their tomorrow".

The climate debate, which is really a proxy for the debate about fiat monetary economics, desperately needs fixing - and in a good way please Mrs Yellen.

All our values are encapsulated in the money we use and a prosperous future will not be served with more "extend and pretend", QE, market interventions and deficit financing with unlimited unsound money.

Donald Dump: how Trump the pottymouth triggered an artistic overload

30 Nov 2015 19:02

Donald Trump proves that US politics is in a state of erectile dysfunction. Add to the mix a dose of senility, and like poor old Hilary Clinton, the aging, drug dependent baby boomers prove a real and present danger to the rest of the world.

That said, only Donald Trump recognises that capitalism cannot be sustainable unless the money is sound, whereas Hilary Clinton is just wheeled out on behalf of Wall St and the Fed.

Pull yourselves together Labour moderates, and stop the sneering

30 Nov 2015 20:33

What on earth is he doing? I thought Jeremy Corbyn was a man of principle who wanted to create positive change in his own image?

By whipping his party he had a golden opportunity to a) make the right moral and strategic decision for the country and b) call out and isolate his blairite opponents from the high moral ground. It was the obvious winning calculus.

To fold so feebly he's let down the party members who got him elected and signalled attack to his opponents elsewhere and in his party. He's crumbled like my aunties old hip. If he won't take the intelligent advice, all that's left to say is: "you're on your fucking own".

Nikkei boss: Financial Times purchase is perfect fit for global, digital expansion

Nikkei and the FT are a perfect fit - they both promote the illusion of free market capitalism.

With the BoJ dominant JGB and stock market player, they are the leading example of how the Central Banks have lost the plausible narrative with which they disguise the key tenant of their existence - they do not mark to market and are immune from losses.

The result is that the system has morphed into a command and control economy - markets are neither free nor fair, the dominant market player preventing true price discovery. In effect, this financial politburo has created a socialist dystopia with a veneer of democracy.

China factory indicator at three-year low

1 Dec 2015 11:09

With only 48 hours until Mr Draghi's latest policy farce, it's time for the inconvenient truth - QE is a dysfunctional and impotent policy.

Allow me to explain, banks haven't and won't lend in size at historical low rates because when they create the inevitable inflationary conditions this will be immediately countered by higher rates. Higher rates, with historically high debt burdens, will bankrupt their customers, and in turn, bankrupt the banks themselves. Mr Draghi is asking them to commit economic suicide which they will not do, even with negative nominal rates.

Debt with a fiat currency doesn't get repaid, meaning the existence of fiat currency is limited by time itself. It's a time bomb system with ever increasing sensitivity and is ensured to fail.

Bombing Isis is not enough – we'll need to talk to them too

1 Dec 2015 08:48

This unhinged individual is actually implying that any group or individual who wants to put forward an alternative idea or narrative needs to start bombing, shooting and killing. Only by this method of shock and awe will the established orthodoxy talk and negotiate.

This is clear incitement to commit acts of violence, although considering his blairite background its not surprising that reasoned argument and debate is a redundant tool?

I'm a tenant, a loser by today's standards. But I won't shut up

1 Dec 2015 09:28

For all the renters and disaffected out there, writing reasoned and logical arguments on the internet or contacting your MP is a complete waste of time and will get you absolutely nowhere.

On this website today, the ex-Govt Chief of Staff, Johnathon Powell admits the government and establishment only negotiate real change with violent organisations - in fact the more vicious and violent the better.

So, if you want to create much needed change in this country your available choices have been made clear, take the instruction of Blair's Chief of Staff , and make it so.

Cameron wins Syria airstrikes vote by majority of 174 – as it happened

2 Dec 2015 15:37

You know when you're on the right side of the argument when the critical issues are swept under the carpet and suppressed. It beggars belief that MP's wont use their parliamentary privilege and bring up all the inconvenient truths around Turkey, oil, Saudi, funding, CIA and US with fingers everywhere, all information publically available.

It is undemocratic at best, cowardly at worst and a damming indictment of the spooked "professional unprincipled politician".

Cameron pressing leaders for EU deal by Christmas, says Tusk

2 Dec 2015 10:04

The PM is panicked, knee-jerking everywhere you look, his mask and narratives slipping like marbles under horses hooves.

All on a day when the UK staggers head long into military conflict using the weakest arguments for war in history.

BBC impartiality 'absolutely critical' as it covers EU referendum, MPs told

3 Dec 2015 13:13

Who's running the training, HSBBC's institutional sales desk?

Steve Bell on Cameron and Syria airstrikes – cartoon

2 Dec 2015 22:30

Congratulations go to the PM, he's had a "right touch". Now only history will expose the true nature of the mistake.

European stocks slide after ECB dashes hopes of major QE expansion

3 Dec 2015 13:20

An investigation of the FT must happen for a clear breach of protocol and market manipulation.
1. Releasing privileged, market sensitive information early.
2. Releasing incorrect information.

Joanna Lumley attacks 'evil' TV gender pay gap

3 Dec 2015 15:29

Using the pejorative "evil" is unbecoming of Mrs Lumley.

Kamal Ahmed to replace Robert Peston as BBC economics editor

3 Dec 2015 23:20

Ahmed is an economic illiterate, fluent only in group think.

Defense secretary will tell US military to open all combat jobs to women

3 Dec 2015 17:35

US make new lows.

David Attenborough says BBC in 'real danger' in face of cuts and online rivals

5 Dec 2015 11:50

The problem with the BBC is that its special pleading is predicated on dishonesty.

Ignore the fact that they, and the govt, claim the war on terror against Islamic State doesn't have a religious context, but more importantly they refuse all discussion about the efficacy of fiat money and economics, yet it's the most universally important subject on earth because everybody uses money.

My opinion, formed over 20 professional years dealing with money, markets and economics, is that fiat money, or money based on unlimited debt, is unfair and unsound, because it is a transference of wealth from the future to the present at the disadvantage of those unable to protect themselves, children and the yet unborn.

For me, it's the most egregious, and some say, deviant scheme imaginable. 100 years ago, prior to the formation of the Federal Reserve, money was a commodity currency, the gold standard, the effect of which was that money was backed with honesty and a morality. The subsequent moral decline is a direct result of the experiment with fractional reserve and then fully unhinged fiat money.

When you understand that all our values and desires are encapsulated in the money we use, you can appreciate that to suppress this societal and moral debate, is the root of all dishonesty and the BBC's greatest weakness. Until they deal honestly with this most universally important subject, their fortunes will continue to flounder.

The airstrikes debate: once more unto the breach – of good taste

6 Dec 2015 12:35

This policy mistake is already having real measurable effects on the ground.

As quick as Phillip Hammond up a drainpipe, property speculating spivs in Cheltenham have been buying up property right across the town. It is based on sound logic.

After getting a peak at the real views of the PM, GCHQ will have to up their game. Given over 50% of the population are terrorist sympathizers, the donut will have to double in size and these people will need housing.

And while I'm at it, I agree with David Mitchell, the speech by Hilary Benn, plumbed new depths of good taste, but when all you want is the power to borrow from the future, the lies build up like bodies on the landing grounds of truth.

Ben Jennings on the San Bernardino shootings – cartoon

7 Dec 2015 13:13

Mr Obama provides the opportunity to bring up the hypocrisy surrounding the ISIS/war/muslim extremism debate.

The PM and fellow group thinkers denounce ISIS as un-Islamic and a perversion of Islam. How do they know and as non-muslims what gives them to right to make such judgements? Surely only a muslim can say whether ISIS is un-Islamic or not. It's like me saying a menstruating woman never feels sexy. Only a woman can confirm whether that is a true or not.

David Cameron attacked for delaying Heathrow expansion decision

7 Dec 2015 22:08

The PM has reached his zenith; it's all downhill for him now.

Gordon Brown to join investment firm Pimco's global advisory board

8 Dec 2015 10:42

Gordon Brown will be presumably advising that higher rates, with fiat currencies, means a tightening of credit conditions and will result in a contraction of economic activity and an unwinding of the asset bubbles.

He's unlikely to admit his gilts, that borrowing from your children and not paying it back is imprudent and akin to financial paedophilia.

Donald Trump's real threat is making extreme bigots seem moderate

8 Dec 2015 18:15

Owen Jones makes some interesting points. Everybody knows David Cameron privately believes that ISIS actually practice the purest form of Islam and in fact others are inferior Muslim's akin to Easter and Christmas Anglicans, or Friday night binge drinkers. If you claim to believe in a set of worded instructions, you either believe them or not.

Maybe the PM will have a sudden attack of candour and attempt to trump the enemy. He claims the West is carrying the torch of enlightenment for the world. He preaches about the scourge of female inequality yet turns a blind eye to an entrenched female submissive patriarchy coupled with medieval face covering. The two positions are immiscible and irreconcilable with rational thought.

The inconvenient truth is that only big business has benefited from the large-scale experiment of mixing oil and water that is Muslim integration with the enlightened western culture.

Tyson Fury has no fear of retribution – he will say and do as he pleases

Mr Fury may be advised to change his narrative towards: "Although I find your lifestyle vile, abhorrent and an affront to nature, in the pursuit of liberty for all, I defend to the death, your right to do it".

Tony Blair bemoans 'tragedy' of Labour under Corbyn

9 Dec 2015 09:45

Why and who at the Guardian is trying to protect Andrew Feldman?

Osborne criticised over Treasury job for former bank lobbyist

9 Dec 2015 17:22

Aside: now we know the real reason for the rushed decision to escalate the war - yesterday's bombshell and polarising IMF announcement allowing Ukraine to default on its Russian debt - things are deteriorating fast.

9 Dec 2015 17:13

You're losing the plot George.

Without Syrians at the front and centre of talks, there can be no lasting peace

10 Dec 2015 13:20

Being long gold has been a tiring trade. While fiat is still in place the Fed and their banks will do everything to suppress its true value. The banks and some large funds are short comex in huge size to keep the benchmark price down.

If people concentrate on getting their representatives to debate and then repeal fiat money, they will be rich and rich enough.

It is naïve at best to believe that peace talks have any relevance at this juncture. The Middle East has already been chosen by military planners as the "theatre of dreams". It looks increasingly likely that the only way out of this dead end the Federal Reserve etal have driven us down is either wide-scale, intercontinental debt default or a further escalation of war.

With the IMF further polarising the battlefield between the dollar and yuan/ruble the best hope for the world is debt default followed by talks agreeing to re-instate the gold standard or similar a incarnation.

Yes, the Tories are deceitful – but I take my hat off to their political sorcery

10 Dec 2015 10:50

I challenge Owen Jones to prove me wrong

10 Dec 2015 10:28

It's a bit rich to single out the Tories for deceit. Every member of Parliament is displaying stratospheric levels of deceit and/or ignorance.

Everyday they surreptitiously spout support for money based on debt, handling a genuine weapon of mass destruction. They justify the system of borrowing from the future, your children, never paying it back, and ensuring rampant inequality.

If you want proof that what I'm saying is true, just try and get any of them, or the media, to deny or discuss it.

Heathrow third runway decision put off until at least summer 2016

11 Dec 2015 09:30

It's been a good week for the PM if you like indecision, incompetence and cronyism.

Cameron's judgement is in tatters and becoming extremely dangerous. He will defend the indefensible like his tennis chum, but can't make a critically important decision affecting the lives of millions of people, that is unless it involves aerial bombardment. I also hesitate to mention the mess he's making in Europe which is risking the country leaving the EU. The inconvenient truth is that he is becoming a national liability.

10 Dec 2015 22:24

I agree with Laura Kuessnberg, Cameron is showing the judgement of a toddler with a broken rattle.

Markets tumble as oil falls; IMF chief Lagarde highlights Brexit risk - as it happened

11 Dec 2015 10:07

You never know, just like she's done with Ukraine, she may announce we can renege on our national debts.

With Islamophobia on the rise I fear for my friends and family

11 Dec 2015 17:18

Islam has been good for Britain if you like isolated ghettoized communities with immiscible and illiberal views.

 Paris climate talks: delegates reach agreement on final draft text

12 Dec 2015 11:50

In response to akardyagain

A commodity currency keeps the worst excesses of human nature in check by limiting its creation to hard work and natural supplies. Money just based on the issuance of more and more debt, is a classic Ponzi scheme, which requires ever more participants, more consumption, more pollution, more of everything, more and quicker climate change to sustain it - can you see?

A commodity currency, such as gold, is Nature's, or if you prefer, God's, money of choice. Without money limited in some way, we cease to be human in nature.

11 Dec 2015 23:33

It seems clear that climate change is a result of fiat economics, globalisation and population increase. If so, the only solution is either death or compromise. Rampant development and population increase can be undone by war but that is merely an admission that humanity is regressing.

How to defeat Donald Trump and his ilk: fight fire with fire

11 Dec 2015 20:07

It might be time to come down off the high wire Mr Cameron, it's starting to fray.

Bridget Christie: Hilary Benn and the trouble with audiences

12 Dec 2015 11:27

In response to HollyGun

I agree, Hilary Benn, like Cameron, is the type who wakes every morning and thanks his blessings for all the poor and ignorant who can't see through his vile, enslaving Ponzi scheme of debt. But the real insult is that Benn does his lying wrapped up in a Labour jacket.

12 Dec 2015 08:55

Only the sickest, most deviant sociopath would get you to conspire against your children. Hilary Benn, like Blair and Cameron, has spent a lifetime promoting unsustainable debt and unsound fiat economics.

What Orwell can teach us about the language of terror and war

12 Dec 2015 15:00

Mr Williams, it hasn't gone unnoticed that you've presided over a litany of failure in the fortunes of the CofE. That trend should really preclude you from further meddling in the future, but in the spirit of liberty and redemption, I wish you a happy retirement.

Majority of students experience mental health issues, says NUS survey

14 Dec 2015 10:50

Organisations and people who are trying to categorise emotions as "mental health issues" should be resisted at all cost. To experience anxiety, apathy, despair, disappointment, disgust, fear, frustration, guilt, hatred, hope, horror, hurt, loneliness, lust, rage, regret, remorse, sadness, shame, sorrow and share is as natural as affection, arousal, confidence, courage, ecstasy, happiness, joy, passion, pleasure, wonder and zest. Those wishing to manipulate your emotions are purposely trying to un-balance you with the main objective being to divert you away from the real prison of the mind, the yoke of debt.

Press turns on David Cameron over his 'pathetic' EU negotiations

14 Dec 2015 11:57

Things are deteriorating fast. The EU negotiators have seen through the spin and bluster and unveiled the PM as a spiv and a chancer. He is finding out the EU representatives aren't quite as gullible as the hordes nodding and dribbling on the green benches.

People don't have to like Hillary Clinton to vote for her. Who likes Donald Trump?

14 Dec 2015 17:17

I'm terribly sorry but Hilary Clinton is away with the birds. Devoid of any vision or principle she just pecks around in the dirt of US politics for a narrative to regurgitate. She is too old, too tarnished, too incompetent and too downright dangerous to become POTUS.

'A spectacular day at the office': rocket successfully reaches ISS - as it happened

15 Dec 2015 12:19

A good, useful propaganda story but of little practical benefit to humanity. All a day before Fed chair Yellen starts to tighten the biggest debt bubble in history. Expect rockets and fireworks down on earth.

Scotland's debt mountain: Holyrood's borrowing could hit £50bn by 2020

15 Dec 2015 16:56

Nicola Sturgeon is the Bernie Madoff of British politics. Borrowing on the back of the next generation, the children she doesn't have, is surely the most deviant and obnoxious behaviour possible?

There is no Nazi gold train, Polish scientists say

I thought it was common knowledge that the Nazi gold is in Rolex.

UK job data: pay growth slows to 2%

16 Dec 2015 11:44

Laissez-faire free markets never fail - crony, manipulated markets have and do fail. Sustainable capitalism can only contain free markets, open to price discovery.

How to run the British government when 'things get sticky'

17 Dec 2015 09:22

I apologise for being a little crude but it has to be said, the PM has been doing a good job of reading the lines given to him by the magic circle in the right order without dribbling or grunting but recently he's started to think his shit smells good - a sure sign of madness and impending doom.

Cameron arrives at EU summit promising to battle for Britain 'right through the night' - Politics live

17 Dec 2015 18:34

Mr Cameron, some friendly advice, the "bullying cad" routine won't work in the EU negotiations tonight, try "sensitive decorum" instead. And by the way, your protégé, the MP for Telford, has gone fully unhinged, you might like to get her seen to ASAP.

Bank of England to be given powers to rein in buy-to-let market

Please, please, please, Mark Carney doesn't your best interests at heart, he works for the banking interests, and against yours. In this case, his job is to manage the banks buy-to-let mortgage exposure.

The Old Lady of Threadneedle St needs to get her house in order, have a good clear out, open some windows and let some fresh, clean air in.

Ukip gently implodes with EU referendum finish line in sight

What really astounds me is that the dark-side Freudian's at the BBC have flip-flopped and are now actually trying to protect Mr Farage. What a perverse country we live in.

The problem at UKIP is the leader, he thinks people haven't noticed, but you can't maintain credibility by un-resigning when you've sobered up the next day. A man of his word doesn't go back on it.

Future of Assad in doubt as UN unanimously supports Syria peace process

It seems clear the biggest problem in the area is Turkey's Erdogen. He is swinging through the trees lying, double-dealing and bullying. This, of course, conceals the weakness of the coward, but nevertheless, nothing can improve with him in office.

Ignore the landlord-martyrs: it's time for the Bank to intervene over buy-to-let

Everyone knows our money, the pound, is a subsidiary of the Federal Reserve's fiat dollar and the fiat dollar is nothing but debt, faux wealth borrowed from the future, or more accurately, from your children. It is inherently unfair and unstable as it is designed as a money funnel to the banking interests and a diminishing number of real asset holders.

The only way to change the trajectory of this missile of mass social destruction is to shoot it down with stinging arguments, starting with warning shots. To change hearts and minds, first you must be prepared to break some hearts. In the absence of a new gold standard, inequality and sustainable social cohesion can only be maintained by dealing with a problem close to home. The price of housing in the UK is a missile out of control. The solution with the least pain is to target the buy to let/private landlords, the rentier class, who are prepared to profit at the expense of those unable to defend themselves. These people must be shown the exit and general prices must be put on a sustainable path. Not acting on this fundamental issue, signals that the BofE is only working on behalf of a shrinking minority and not in the interests of the whole country. Over to you Mr Carney.

Clinton sets sights on Republicans with eye to general election campaign

21 Dec 2015 11:44

Hilary Clinton doesn't deal in truth when lies will do.

BBC hires Gus O'Donnell firm to review £700m costs of over-75s' licence fees

21 Dec 2015 11:33

Whatever next - a new re-jigged PFI contract for the BBC devised by the children of wrath.

21 Dec 2015 09:12

The magic circle at work - the BBC dark-side freudians hate free markets when cronyism will do.

Rome won't be rebuilt in a day: the challenge of city centre restoration

21 Dec 2015 11:15

I presume this article is really about Ukraine's default on it Russian euro bond. This must leave Russia in no doubt that the purpose of US foreign policy is simply to feed the military industrial complex.

Sepp Blatter and Michel Platini banned from football for eight years by Fifa

21 Dec 2015 20:25

It is unsurprising that Sepp Blatter is seething with incredulity over his "outing" when he has seen the depths of corruption swimming just beneath the surface of global business and institutions. The FBI could be playing with fire here, he seems the type, if cornered, would spill the beans on the whole shebang.

Sepp Blatter press conference: 'I have become a punching bag for Fifa'– as it happened

21 Dec 2015 10:37

The BBC is literally frothing with vested interests and prejudice over toppling Sepp Blatter. The BBC accusing Blatter of corruption is like Hitler accusing Churchill of anti-Semitism.

High street retailers hope for last-minute rush of Christmas shoppers

21 Dec 2015 12:44

Let the Proles have a "sale" for Christmas.

Murdoch at the centre of power again as Cameron drops round for drinks

21 Dec 2015 21:28

How many times, the PM can't do any thinking for himself. He still believes the way to solve the EU problem is to get the European Jonnies hooked on cricket.

Besieged Afghan forces in Sangin receive airdrops as UK sends troops

22 Dec 2015 09:24

British foreign policy, under the direction of the US, is going really well if you like feeding the military industrial complex with endless, unwinnable wars, against ideas and other invisible enemies. Only the Children of Wrath would welcome such a state of affairs.

Japan set to unveil expansionary budget

22 Dec 2015 09:11

Kuroda's madness will fall foul of life lesson No1: "you can't con an honest man."

What's the point of EU referendum debate if ministers are muzzled?

22 Dec 2015 09:57

A successful referendum debate is far more likely with Jenkins firmly muzzled and tied up on a double tight leash to stop him trying to hump the furniture.

Tory MP criticises party chairman over pro-EU fundraising

22 Dec 2015 18:10

Feldman's name has been blackened, his character besmirched, but according to the PM, that makes him even more suitable for the position as Conservative Party Chairman. Well, that sort of logic may be acceptable in CCHQ but out in the real world, they are harming the price of Sterling, becoming a laughing stock and by extension, a national liability.

Only Saudi Arabia can defeat Isis

22 Dec 2015 12:25

ISIS is the Saudi Arabian expeditionary force.

Does a nose job hurt? You asked Google – here's the answer

23 Dec 2015 12:12

Fixing the nose of this attractive Lady gives an opportunity to bring up the much maligned subject of group think in UK society. The power of group think has allowed nonsense and subjective opinion to be passed off as fact, such as conflating debt with wealth, or happiness with money. The leaders of group think are the highest perceived moral authority in the land which until recently has been the BBC. Group think controls, subconsciously, acceptable thought. For example, if someone were to say "The Jews are predisposed to greed and financial manipulations due to a superiority complex" social conditioning would cause instant recoil as the remark would immediately offend the senses and sensibilities. Group think results in a narrowing band of acceptable thoughts and opinions within the population, to the point, where everybody thinks the same thing, at the same time, when the correct stimuli is given.

The Freudians at the BBC would argue that the animals need to be kept in their designated pens to prevent them from escaping and ruining the order of the farm but those who hold a higher opinion of the general population believe as intelligent animals we should be at liberty to explore all corners of the mind, perception, and understanding as long as it is done peacefully. If members of society can't think independent or creative thoughts how do we progress as a species, in effect, we cease to be human in nature.

I'm married to a man but attracted to women. What should I do?

24 Dec 2015 17:17

The perils of using HRT on the farm.

2016: The year of living precariously

27 Dec 2015 09:11

It's no good playing dead, everyone can see you!

Supressing the important news - that the Swiss are holding a referendum on whether banks should be allowed to create money from debt - just signals that you want to protect the banking cartel which increases inequality and creates faux wealth by borrowing from your children. Your position is indefensible.

Dutch city plans to pay citizens a 'basic income', and Greens say it could work in the UK

27 Dec 2015 10:13

This Government has literally gone insane.

Hard to sum up the magnitude of this nonsense in a sentence other than showing you how their creditability is shot through. They find a bit of paper, print a number on it, and give it you to spend - mad money. With unlimited money no problem can ever exist, want a new hospital – you can have it, want a new car – the government can give you free money to buy it – The government has just declared itself the omnipotent, unquestioned God, Deorum Dao– accountable to no one, believing in nothing, making the laws it keeps, rigging everything in sight - a real life full corruption, authoritarian dystopic reality.

Oliver Letwin blocked help for black youth after 1985 riots

30 Dec 2015 08:22

Of course Oliver Letwin holds these views. But be under no illusion, this is constructed news, a false flag diversion to get the proles frothing over something other than the PM's similar, yet more tactful, incompetence.

IMF chief Lagarde warns of disappointing global growth in 2016 – as it happened

30 Dec 2015 14:04

Those who instigated, and now perpetuate, the failed experiment of unsound fiat money have corralled us into a dead end.

Now, when they claim that "borrowing from your children with no intention of repaying" or "the basis for prosperity is being calling into question" you know these people are morally and intellectually bankrupt.

30 Dec 2015 10:44

Aren't we all lucky we don't live under the medieval Taliban where criticism of policy and theory is discouraged.

In the enlightened West we can openly point out our financial system is fundamentally flawed, that our (fiat) money is just debt, faux wealth borrowed from our children, and that our new double-deviant QE funny money is just unbridled money printing, direct financing of public deficits and full monetization of the next generations future for the benefit of baby-boomers today.

'Revenge is not very Jedi': warning over Labour reshuffle talk

30 Dec 2015 11:55

The blairites are like cross-bred GMO crops or diseased lab rats - an experiment gone badly wrong which can't be reversed. A cull is the only humane thing to do which would allow the herd to be re-stocked .

When there is disease in the herd, all farmers know that they must conduct a cull of those which are ill, frothing at the mouth, or walking around in circles. Hilary Benn represents all those states, so for the good of the party he must be put down, so to speak.

The Guardian view on the New Year honours: cranky, compromised but still useful

31 Dec 2015 08:38

Things are going really well if you like moral, religious and cultural decline. Britain is literally regressing before our eyes. Unsound money, and the deception required to maintain it, have created the conditions for corruption, cronyism and cultural depravity to flourish and grow.

Those presiding over this depravity should be ashamed of themselves.

Are you part of the dreaded metropolitan elite? Do this quiz and find out

31 Dec 2015 10:13

When the highest ideals are promoted people naturally migrate towards them. The moral and cultural landscape is merely a reflection of our leaders. Cameron is a world leader in hypocrisy, cronyism and thinly veiled corruption.

He is signalling that to get on in Britain today you've got to be prepared to lie, cheat and gouge; corrupt, bribe or coerce your way to ill gotten gains. No deception too big, no lie too small, as Draghi says "whatever it takes, whatever the cost". It's no wonder supports Turkey's Erdogan and Hilary Clinton.

It looks like the PM is striving tirelessly to achieve peak corruption in the world today.

Barbara Windsor and Siân Phillips made dames in honours list

31 Dec 2015 09:20

Things are going really well if you like moral, religious and cultural decline. Britain is literally regressing before our eyes. Unsound money, and the deception required to maintain it, have created the conditions for corruption, cronyism and cultural depravity to flourish and grow.

Those presiding over this depravity should be ashamed of themselves.

Why opinion pollsters failed to predict overall majority for David Cameron

31 Dec 2015 17:33

Opinion polling is primitive propaganda. Pollsters are just weather makers, tipsters and touts with vested interests. You can get any answer you want with the correctly worded question.

Q: Should David Cameron be allowed to have Swan and Chips for dinner on New Years Eve?

Sports Direct pledges £10m towards staff pay rise

31 Dec 2015 21:02

The Sword of Damocles hangs over the stock markets as well as Ashley. The question is will the horse's hair hold? The hive of emotions at the home of National Hunt tomorrow may hold some clues.

UK in 'one of the great reforming decades', says David Cameron

1 Jan 2016 10:57

Pseudo intellectuals, like guardian readers and writers, think they are clever but most don't even understand the thing they value most, money. They know not where it comes from, who controls it and how it shapes the values of everybody who use it. Instead of walking around in a state of ignorance, understand what enslaves generations in debt and inequality. It will benefit you and society as a whole.

Obama to meet with Loretta Lynch to discuss 'epidemic of gun violence'

1 Jan 2016 18:08

America is literally regressing before our eyes, Clinton, Bush, Obama, a triptych of failure, hypocrisy and cronyism. Their moral and philosophical standing disintegrating in perfect correlation to the soundness of their fiat dollar.

Justin Welby's message on refugees is a clarion call for a better, bigger Britain

1 Jan 2016 15:07

As a property hedge fund manager and supporter of unsustainable debt and unsound money, Justin Welby is a leader in his field.

'House of Morgan': a Chinese mogul, an anti-capitalist artist and an icon of Wall St

2 Jan 2016 13:03

The only thing in the vault today is a photocopier and the misery of future generations.

US presidential election 2016: the state of the Democratic race as the year starts

2 Jan 2016 12:45

The Democrats are in desperate trouble for the simple reason that they cannot reconcile their desire for peace and equality with the goals of it's leadership.

The way to ensure world peace is to have many small, individual countries, co-operating and competing together. The Clinton's, and

I suspect the BBC and Guardian, want a single world government, translated, this means they want to rule the entire world themselves, creating the monopolies, picking the winners, sacrificing the losers, in their own deviant image.

Every step down that road would bring us closer to an inevitable tyranny and enslavement. Do you really want to continue that journey?

I won't join the Letwin lynch mob. We need a more serious discussion on race

3 Jan 2016 11:27

Trevor Philips is a great chap if you like unprincipled political types who only ever make a stink in the bathroom each morning. He is symptomatic of the self-serving, deceptive thinking, which 40 years ago, bought us unsound fiat money: Do you want to live within your means under a moral authority or do you want to enslave your children in debt, never pay them back and ensure rampant widening inequality? They chose the indefensible option of financial paedophilia.

That's one reason why I'm full of hope for the reign of King Charles, you can tell from his initiatives that he appreciates the argument that money should be limited in nature.

Health warnings can be bad for you. Risk brings us together

3 Jan 2016 21:05

I like the way Zoe Williams strings her words together, it shows a depth of thought and a zest for life.

You're a performance artist in the same vein as a talented $20 hooker, both gaping with hypocrisy and self-hate.

The Conservative Gang are under severe pressure as the truth leaks out like a torn colostomy bag. Adding to their wows, the sleeper cell who infiltrated the Labour Gang, including agent Benn, are about to get castrated. When the animal gets cornered I'd expect a violent and badly thought out response.

Scottish culture secretary accused of preposterous claims about BBC spending

4 Jan 2016 12:00

Big Sister must be worried, Sturgeon's henchwoman certainly has an air of violence about her, she looks the type who could do a bottle of vodka and it wouldn't touch the sides.

Dogged enforcers: the well-trained social media world of Dogspotting

3 Jan 2016 20:52

More evidence that animals revert to type. The author is literally running with the press-pack. Unfortunately all this barking is unbecoming and unnecessary.

Beware, the central control that grips schools is heading universities' way

4 Jan 2016 08:39

When the whole system is predicated on deceit these problems will be just the tip of the iceberg. If you continue to teach and preach unsound economics, such as conflating debt with wealth, the system will continue to lurch from crisis to crisis.

The bottom line is that money without limit creates problems without solution. Money should be limited in nature.

War and Peace review – this compellingly silly Russian saga is just a bit too English

4 Jan 2016 09:37

Big Sister, formally known as Big Brother, has a major problem. The BBC has misjudged the mood of the British public and their ability to wade through the misinformation and diversions. Coverage of Islamic State is a case in point. Ignoring the fact that giving these medieval savages any more than a passing comment is tantamount to collaborating with the enemy, predicating the coverage of their little videos with the words "propaganda" is counter-productive.

All it does is highlight that the BBC has no confidence in the viewer or listener to disseminate between their "bad" propaganda and the BBC's "good" propaganda, ultimately the strength of their own arguments. Propaganda is just the presentation of ideas, in the same way that a female wears lipstick or high heels to attract a mate, putting a gloss on the bare bones of the thing, so to speak. To thrive in this brave new world the BBC need to start trusting its audience and stop treating them like captured enemy combatants.

What will it take to build George Osborne's 400,000 homes?

4 Jan 2016 10:38

It would take a dissolution of all vested interests such as in the banks, house building companies and property speculators. In a word it would take the government to turn away from the dark side, a miracle.

American football is too dangerous, and it should be abolished

Obama's government calling for calm in the middle east is like an arsonist calling for fire engines.

Boris Johnson urged to disinvest from bank linked to Saudi regime

4 Jan 2016 18:27

The rationale for doing such a transaction is highly questionable or down right corrupt. Both banks operate under sharia law and therefore don't charge interest on money. This is in direct conflict with the principles of capitalism, so he is either collaborating with an enemy of Judaeo-Christian monetary principles or the funds are used for other nefarious purposes. Either way, Londoners deserve to know. Well done Mr Fallon.

HSBC customers vent fury over online banking disruption

5 Jan 2016 11:30

The Sword of Damocles for Fiat Economics

The economic, social and moral basis for fiat money is broken beyond repair.

Capitalism represents the market place for money. History tells us that it is the most efficient way of bringing savers and borrowers together. The more efficient and free the market the tighter the spread of prices received or paid. This spread constitutes the health of capitalism. Capitalism is unwell but not the problem, the money we use is.

Fiat money has been in existence for just over 44 years. Let's take a look at some facts. Interest rates represent a) the cost of money for borrowers or the price paid to savers b) the health (or confidence)

of the system from the point of view of the banks. When fiat interest rates are high, so is the banks confidence in its money. When interest rates are low, so is confidence.

Interest rates are currently at all-time lows.

Savers can't make a real return and in some cases are actually paying, in both nominal and real terms, to deposit money in banks. For savers fiat money has no value.
Borrowers fare differently depending on who they are.
Governments: Central banks, such as the Swedish Riksbank, are now actually paying Governments to borrow their money. The bank's fiat money has a negative value; they can't give it away to Government. This phenomenon is known as negative rates, and it represents the fact that confidence in fiat money has never been lower.
Corporates: Depending on the size, the banks have been prepared to give its money away for free (0%) or at a small cost.
Individuals: Despite base rates being zero or even negative, the cost of money to individuals can vary dramatically from around 4% to levels of usury exceeding 1000%.
Take-away: The perceived credit-worthiness between individuals and Gov't/Big Business has never been wider.

So what are these facts telling us?
Fiat money is bad for savers
Fiat money is good for big business and Government.
Fiat money is very bad for consumers.
Fiat money is destroying Free market Capitalism.

Fiat money is run by the central banks for the benefit of themselves. Politicians have to answer the following question: Should monetary economics be run for the benefit of a few banks, businesses and governments or for the billions of individuals populating the earth?

Propaganda is but the presentation of an idea, which may include analysis, supposition and fact. Everybody is using propaganda of varying degrees and effectiveness. For example, the PM must have used a whole barrel load to convince Samantha to marry him. It is ubiquitous. The BBC have made a career of it. To call IS videos propaganda is true in the same way as a party political broadcast. The difference is stark in that only one promote direct violence. Arguments can be formed for the purpose of good or bad, which although subjective, just represents a myriad of all minded considerations. I consider something good if it benefits all rather than a few. Propaganda can good, bad or desperate.

Don't bet against deflation's return

5 Jan 2016 15:55

Deflation is flooding in on half empty Chinese container ships.

Labour reshuffle continues with no news on future of Hilary Benn

5 Jan 2016 20:18

If Hilary Benn doesn't go, JC will have developed an outstanding trend for creating chaos out of order.

John McDonnell: Labour reshuffle will end frontbench dissent

6 Jan 2016 10:42

Incompetence reigns over the House of Commons. This is a recipe for a disaster. A weak PM opposed by an even weaker individual with a gift for creating chaos out of order. Who said we weren't ruled by the least among us.

Jeremy Corbyn's minor reshuffle could have major repercussions

6 Jan 2016 11:50

With a motto of "Chaos out of Order", only industrial strength electro therapy could balance Jeremy Corbyn's mind.

The most moving thing about Obama's tears was witnessing his inner struggle

6 Jan 2016 16:13

Obama is a consummate professional, a truly great actor, he's like Washington's version of The Duke in Escape from New York.

George Osborne has tied a knot of fear and optimism – but is it unravelling?

7 Jan 2016 13:33

Open letter to David Cameron 7th Jan 2016

Dear David

I hope your well.

Look, it's time for a bit of honesty. We both know that all the public's problems are rooted in the same thing – unsound money and the consequences it sows – playing the public like fools has been successful for the last few years but I must tell you I fear the game is up.

People want money they can trust. They understand that honest money creates a certainty, a confidence to plan, to invest, to prosper. Dishonest money breeds mistrust of authority, of information, of others, of the future.

People are sick and tired of unsound money, money just printed on paper and thrown around like confetti backed by nothing but debt, lies and rampant inequality. It is strangling all confidence in the future.

We know that money which is sound is backed by a universal truth not a set of lies, that's why the Gold Standard provided stability and prosperity for centuries. People have no reason to trust a fiat government; they would prefer to trust themselves and society as a whole. The link between the government control of money and its supply must be de-coupled by making it sound and limited in nature. It will improve both government, citizens and their mutual relationship. Only the 1% uber rich and the mega banks will be affected but they can cope and adapt like all good businesses and individuals.

For the alternative, all we need to do is decide what we value within nature and limit our money to its use. Money without limit creates problems without solution, it is inhuman in nature and the time is right to end the experiment and walk away as better and wiser men.
Go out and use these words to create the change that all desire.

Yours faithfully
Tom Naysburn

Saudi Arabia considers IPO for national oil group, Aramco

8 Jan 2016 11:15

The House of Saud are just old time sex slavers and caravan bandits who have had some influential friends. They are nothing but a paper tiger and need to buy some vested interests quick smartish. Appealing to greed is really a sign of desperation.

The House of Saud is howling to the world that it wants more friends than just a couple of intelligence agencies.

'Mega Mao' no more as ridiculed golden statue destroyed

8 Jan 2016 12:50

If the communist party want to disassociate themselves with gold they should take off their wedding rings and hand in their jewellery.

Andrew Tyrie blasts 'out of touch' Office for National Statistics

8 Jan 2016 13:47

All individuals who aren't directly responsible for their own income suffer from some degree of political influence. The domesticated animal looks to his master for food. The influence of the master is inversely correlated to the availability of alternative food sources, just ask Mark Carney. The ONS are fully domesticated and captured.

Cameron could extend tax credits ban to British expats to reach EU deal

9 Jan 2016 11:42

The PM has no direction because there is nothing he wants to achieve. That's the problem with privilege; it's a double edged sword. A leader by privilege, or a privileged leader, that is the question. Those born into leadership have never experienced a struggle except from protecting their privilege from others. The result is a lack of moral and ethical fibre. Without a moral compass the leader by privilege will just drift directionless and without destination. As long as his or her privilege is secured success can be rationalised. This is the state of Britain a council of despair.

War and Peace is a hit. But Britain can't keep living in the past

Central Banks and their Governments use unsound fiat money to steal the future but they want you to live in the past. A sustainable future only exists by living in the present with sound money.

The left must admit the truth about the assaults on women in Cologne

9 Jan 2016 09:33

The truth is that the PM was complicit in the decision to allow thousands of military aged enemy combatants holding illiberal and immiscible views into the EU.

It is so unbelievable the motives of the likes of Peter Sutherland must be questioned.

Russian bombing in Syria 'fuels refugee crisis' says US official as airstrike kills 39

9 Jan 2016 14:52

So much questionable activity has come to light, conducted by this president and his controllers, that the US has lost all credible moral authority. What a state of affairs.

Treasury interference in Polish media? That sounds just like the BBC

10 Jan 2016 10:15

The BBC is fundamentally compromised as an organisation. To be truly confidence about anything in life, an argument, a skill, a relationship or whatever, you must first have explored the possibility that you're wrong.

The likes of Andrew Neil talk the flat earth economic orthodoxy with an arrogant certainty, but it's clear they don't even understand the thing they love most, money. The result is a contemptible barrage of banking propaganda delivered by an organisation retarded by the gluttony of a trust fund. They don't respect money because they've never needed to earn any.

Until this changes, the public will continue to be played like fools.

As Mein Kampf returns to Germany, the world is again awash with hatred

11 Jan 2016 18:41

Mr Mason, you can't undo the damage you've helped promote but it isn't too late to join the Pre-Raphaelites. The Enlightenment doesn't have membership cards; brothers and sisters work silently, crashing through the lies, resisting waves of tyranny with truth, rewarding those who see beauty in more than just themselves, promoting liberty and sound money to create a sustainable future for all, grounded in nature.

Is Britain a nation of debt bingers? History tells a different story

12 Jan 2016 12:53

Now I know why Tiger mums sometimes eat their young.

Debt is not wealth, debt can be very dangerous and should be entered into in full cognizance.

Why the new women and work all-party parliamentary group matters

13 Jan 2016 09:46

A leader, either male or female, inspires others through their actions and successes. MP's want to lead, I presume, because they are enthused to create change in society using the ideology with which they have been convinced. I'm an enthusiastic supporter of equality but I have to say some with such vested interests are giving off the air of cult members.

People whose sole purpose is to achieve equal numbers in every strata are actually doing a disservice to young women. Leaders must be more than one trick ponies, they must inspire through success in multiple fields, showing the market place of ideas that they understand the problems and are fully equipped to deal with them. Just saying that equal numbers, regardless of ability, will suffice, is actually the council of mediocrity and despair. The premise has been set that your sex cannot restrict you so it is up to women to show leadership through the inspiration of their ideas and solutions.

Obama's message of hope over hate is an example to us all

13 Jan 2016 13:10

They say all great fortunes come from someone somewhere stealing something from somebody else, Obama and the Clinton's have done it by enslaving future generations in a bondage of debt and rampant inequality.

Stealing the future from those unable to defend themselves is possibility the lowest trick of all.

DiCaprio leads a star-studded cast for World Economic Forum in Davos

13 Jan 2016 20:59

If Justin Welby is questioning his faith, a trip to the money temple with the dark lord Martin Sorrell, is both disturbing and remarkable news just broken by The Guardian.

Bank of England keeps interest rates on hold

14 Jan 2016 17:17

Has the Fed's Bullard just let out the whelp of a dying animal? His latest outpouring is a signal the Fed is fighting for it's life, it's dammed if it does, it's dammed if it doesn't. The cover has been blown and it can't compete with the complete control of the PBOC.

BT's £12.5bn EE takeover gets green light

15 Jan 2016 11:37

The competition and markets authority is nothing of the sort, it has been infiltrated by big business monopoly merchants. As Adam Smith said, the role of good government is to break all concentrations of power to allow free markets to operate efficiently and prosper. Unfortunately, this is just more proof that government has been captured.

Tim Peake spacewalk: astronauts back inside ISS after helmet leak - live

15 Jan 2016 14:04

A vacuous trip onto the roof to repair a solar panel - anything to distract the proles from the pyramid scheme of financial paedophilia back on the ground.

Trump fires Twitter broadside against Cruz as Republican rivals' feud escalates

Trump is right, Cruz and Clinton, are owned by Goldman, like a pair of hamsters in a cage.

If you value your future, neither should be POTUS.

Ted Cruz isn't presidential material, but not because of where he was born

Think of Trump as a Golden Retriever compared to Hilary as an arthritic Poodle crossed with a drooling Pitbull.

'If we want Germans to accept Arabs, Arabs must also learn to accept them'

Please, please, please stop calling these muslims Arabs. You are just signalling to the world that there is something you want hidden.

The Observer view on the next US president

Let's be fair, Clinton represents a dirty and failed past, of impeachment, war, fraud, murder, inequality, cronyism, unsound money, need I go on. You have to admit this background of corruption has left a void which Trump has walked through. He is also lucky, the dark forces of Gov't would I'm sure like to conduct a spectacular to focus the public mind but this would now play directly into Trump's narrative.

In addition, the mainstream media is in disarray, they are resistant to all change and promote the continuation of failed policies, of unsound ponzi scheme economics, borrowing today's wealth from their children, enslaving them in debt, ensuring rampant inequality just so they can continue living their gilded and disconnected lives in which ever ghetto they come from. They have lost the respect and trust of the public which further plays into the hands of Trump.

The zookeepers are finding that the animals have broken their cages and are turning on their captors.

Australian Open 2016: Watson crashes out against Babos – live!

18 Jan 2016 11:15

You have to question the wisdom of breaking this supposition through the damp rag that is Buzzfeed. It just signals to everyone that it is a front for the intelligence services.

Tennis is like the financial markets, corrupt to the core. When individuals see the gov't acting like a crime syndicate it percolates down to all levels. To fix a market which is determined by your own hand requires only greed and a crooked nature. This is a perfect example of why Gov't has a moral responsible which is currently sadly lacking.

Cameron's alienated the very people he must ally with: Muslim women

18 Jan 2016 12:43

Islam has been great for Britain if you like alienated communities holding illiberal and immiscible views.

Cameron's alienated the very people he must ally with: Muslim women

18 Jan 2016 12:31

You can hold any view you like so long it is that of the censor - the tyranny of the weak-minded.

NHS chief demands political consensus on funding elderly and social care

18 Jan 2016 12:17

Simon Stevens is right, sound money and economics is the only way - over to you Mr Carney, playing mute is no longer a strategy.

IMF cuts global growth forecasts

19 Jan 2016 11:18

There is nothing inherently wrong with being wealthy but when some uber rich design a financial system which funnels wealth to them and those in the know at the expense of everyone else and future generations, well that is beyond acceptable. At the current rate it will only take a another decade or so before the entire wealth of the whole world will be captured in just a few hands. Full tyranny will then be a complete certainty.

It only takes a few people to conduct a confidence trick, a con for the less initiated, but if the tell is believable enough the lies can corrupt everything in its path. The banking conn: the Federal Reserve, fractional reserve and finally the fully unhinged fiat money, was started by a few bakers etal but has infected the world.

The gatekeepers of accepted truth, the mainstream media, are the group holding this confidence trick together. The game is up, and the way this years Davos cabal is covered will be enlightening. The individual actions of the media are being closely watched, scorecards marked, to determine who's who and where each individual stands.

Kofi Annan: Vote, make some noise and use your power as a consumer

Let's have a look around the farm and the lie of the land. The term globalisation really means the growth of multinational monopolistic companies and the desire for a global government.

Ever since the Chinese agreed to become the factory of the world, The US has made nothing but confidence tricks and big government. Although this has been on the rise in Europe, the French to their credit still make some beautiful things and the Germans also make stuff, but in the UK we are stuck in the middle, acting as an American forward operating base, unable to control our own defensive weapons, making nothing but surveillance equipment while trying to infect the world with dollar denominated fiat debt from the City of London.
The result of unsound money and placing power in a decreasing number of hands is that we are approaching a zenith of complete corruption.

To save ourselves from full tyranny we need a Monetary Convention, a Truth and Reconciliation Commission as a matter of urgency. Who, amongst our esteemed leaders will step forward and save the world?

Government borrowing lower than expected in December, figures show

22 Jan 2016 13:00

Nobody likes a hypocrite. The gold rings worn by Obama, Cameron and Draghi etal signal to the world a physical manifestation of their deepest love. Knowing something of the wives concerned, this assumption may or may be true, but hypocrisy is corrupting, unvirtuous and ultimately self-defeating. Why wear a useless commodity if they care nothing for it?

For everyone in doubt over the nature of their love, they can send their unwanted rings to Thomas Naysburn c/o Zanadome, Berwick Upon Tweed, England, and replace them with a paper cut out.

World stock markets bounce back after turbulent week

22 Jan 2016 12:21

Some in the mainstream who are begging for more "money printing" are really just signalling to the general public that central banks are panicking and burning the papers like Bernie Madoff.

Total Betting Overload: the scourge of sport and its captive audience

22 Jan 2016 16:37

It's all well and good to sneer at the poor and ignorant but the PM himself is the biggest gambler in the entire country. The fiat money system is a huge gamble, the City of London is the mecca of gambling, the entire economy of the country has been gambled on the housing market. When you gamble the future for wealth today it can hardly be a surprise the principle infects all areas of the society. Don't tell them, but the UK could be legitimately smeared with the tag of "the world's most degenerate gambler".

The author is in fact the worst of all gamblers, one in complete denial of his actions.

Millions prepare for potentially 'paralyzing' east coast winter storm

23 Jan 2016 09:33

The American people might have to get used to bad weather, the president has just requested and been granted authorisation for military action against ISIS in perpetuity across the globe.

Permanent war against an idea is clearly cover and tyrannical in nature, no wonder the American people don't trust the Washington establishment. The US used to lead through example, now, because of unsound fiat $ economics, they lead through threat and fear, surely a sign of a non existent moral authority

The Beeb gets tea and biscuits instead of a grilling at Holyrood

23 Jan 2016 17:05

Power corrupts completely, isn't that the truth; power without accountability ensures complete corruption.

Let's look at the news, they think they are the gatekeepers of accepted thought, the head group thinker, just as Orwell said, but what they dispense on the hour, ever hour is regressing to the lowest common denominator. Some might say it is poisoned flour, other may just call it propaganda, but if the goal is to keep the country dumbed down and pig ignorant they are doing a good job.

Add to the mix the questionable promotion of other deviance recently considered unacceptable such as destroying beauty and truth at the hands of the technocracy which is set to benefit only the few at the expense of the many and you get the picture that this organisation is running rampant over the future. The BBC camera is an out of control Darlek shooting all the wrong people indiscriminately. The Government need to get a grip of this "farmer" before the "animals" start rebelling at the door of the farmhouse.

The BBC is an ugly organisation. No matter how many dead eyed sharks Big Sister get out infront of the Darlek, the truth of the agenda is dark and deviant.

In need of an affordable home? Turn left at Pluto

24 Jan 2016 11:48

Stewart should stop bullying Cameron, the PM can't do vision or hope. The last time he did "blue skies thinking" he came up with idea of opening the tunnels and sewers of London to solve the housing crisis.

Cameron is rudderless, a mere crisis management consultant for the banking interests. He'll be working on things like how to spin the news that "El Chapo" Guzman is Rona Fairhead's biggest client at HSBC.

'Hillary, can you excite us?': The trouble with Clinton and young women

24 Jan 2016 14:11

 "People who continue to work after earning more than they could possibly spend in their lifetimes are power crazed sociopaths, which should preclude them from the political process. Unfortunately these people, the globalist monopoly merchants, also own the media and the politicians. The remaining majority really need someone or something to represent their interests, like a People's Liberty Party. "

Depending on your point of view, that is either a genius idea or inspired thinking from Jill Abramson

British government and Bill Gates announce £3bn to fight malaria

25 Jan 2016 09:13

Without careful handling George is predisposed to go wrong at any turn. Riding with known Trojan horsemen is inauspicious.

Donald Rumsfeld releases solitaire app

25 Jan 2016 12:51

Donald Rumsfeld has a mind like a dirty toilet bowl.

Why the public should know when ministers meet media chiefs

25 Jan 2016 11:42

Some friendly advice Roy, you might like to inform your "students" that in London, £100 will buy you a choice of quite acceptable prostitute's, so imagine what £1m could buy amongst the avaricious alcoholics who populate other distinguished trades such as the House of Commons or the media?

Painting the Modern Garden: Monet to Matisse review – thrillingly cosmic

25 Jan 2016 19:57

"A thing of beauty is a joy forever it will never pass into nothingness" and so on and so forth.

Stock markets slide again; Mark Carney faces MPs - business live

26 Jan 2016 10:17

They say that Government is just a reflection of ourselves - Anyone prepared to borrow on the backs of their children without any intention of repaying is a despicable individual and not worth of any respect – what an ugly pig in a cage.

Could someone please fire off this truth missile to Mr Draghi: "Bad banks don't just exist on paper"

George Osborne appoints Andrew Bailey as FCA chief

26 Jan 2016 11:01

Be under no illusions the debt Ponzi scheme that is our financial system has not been reformed, in fact it is increasingly unstable. Plans are in place, bail-ins, to bail out the banks once again. Government has been fully captured by the banking interests. If they tell you the way is up, it is down; turn right, then go left, peak corruption has arrived. They will skim your bank accounts, your pension and your lifestyle itself before they suffer any pain themselves.

The rational individual has to prepare for an event and withdraw consent, it is state sponsored incompetence.

Cocky Osborne may miss out on top job because of his character flaws

26 Jan 2016 16:51

I think you might be right Mr White.

Lets look at the Tory paddock: George, who has failed on every conceivable economic measure and after his latest outpouring now needs a cattle-prod strength dose of electro-therapy to balance his mind; Boris Johnson, an unsound laughing stock and certified buffoon, which they think makes him perfect to cover up the unsound money; and Theresa May, the type who dreams of going on holiday to Diego Garcia to do some off balance sheet torturing. What a state of affairs

Green party appeals to BBC over decision to deny it broadcast time

26 Jan 2016 18:00

Please, please, please, for the final time, the BBC does not report the news, it tries to make the news. They are trying to construct your reality.

Australian support for monarchy has grown as debate for republic revived

27 Jan 2016 10:33

There are many ways to signal, birds do it in tweets, lions do it in roars. The distinguished constitutionalist Vernon Bognor said that if the Monarch doesn't signal effectively it leaves a void which dark thoughts can populate and grow.

If Australia really is our mirror, it appears to shows signs of doubt. I suspect they want reassurance that the road ahead doesn't involve detours away from sustainable finances, moral certainties and the preservation of nature. Should this be true, it would be easy to put down rebellions by ball brained republicans in places such as the Guardian.

London has become the 'dark star' of Britain. We need to control its success

28 Jan 2016 10:52

Helen Lewis makes some good points.

The financial extortion highlighted by the students is a glimpse at the symptoms caused by fiat money. This is what you get when you build on unsound foundations.

London is like one huge bank, selling nothing but debt. Be under no illusion, banks are debt shops, promoting a debt based monetary system modelled on a ponzi scheme. It is fundamentally unstable. It can only exist if the debt bubble continually grows. This bubble feeds into rising asset prices, such as property, until eventually all the real assets will be held by a tiny minority.

On the present course, fiat money, the banking system, and London itself, is only sustainable if you're prepared to accept a full banking tyranny and complete enslavement.

Truth, Beauty

Beauty, Truth

Truth is Beauty

Beauty and Truth

Truth and Beauty

Beauty is Truth

So forth shall it be so

James Murdoch returns as Sky chairman

29 Jan 2016 12:21

How will Mr Murdoch be dealing with fiat money and economics on Sky? He might like to acquaint himself with some facts:

A Ricochet on the Pyramid of Truth (www.zanadome.com)

The Fiat Money System is broken beyond repair.

For the last 42 years the American banks have forced on the world the financial "experiment" of fiat economics, or debt based money. In the banking business, debt is known as paper. Fiat money is issued and controlled by the major banks and their central banks. They are given the authority to so by Government and the Law. Paper money differs from sound money, such as commodity backed money, because it is created rather than earned. Every time a new loan is made, new fiat money is created. The supply of fiat money is the supply of new debt.

Debt, be that loans, mortgages or bonds, is spending today the future effort which will be spent repaying it; the principle is a distortion of time, debt is like borrowing the future today.

Be under no illusion, the mechanics behind fiat money are that of a pyramid scheme. Its survival is predicated on constantly adding additional layers of new debt. By controlling the issuance of new loans, primarily through interest rates, the banks control the asset bubbles the new money creates. Just like a pyramid scheme the job of the banker is to convincing people to borrow, to spend today what they do not have, to be paid back in the future. Ponzi schemes work until new entrants dry up, in this case, the banks run out of people to lend to. When debt bubbles implode, the price of assets fall.

When the loans went bad in 2007/8, to save themselves, instead of taking their medicine, the central banks slashed the cost, or interest rate, of money, creating fresh money in an attempt to prop up the price of assets already bought and the scheme itself. Fast forward to today and Abe's arrow has just ricocheted against the pyramid of truth, interest rates in Japan are now negative, and the banks have been forced to pay debtors to take new loans.

Look at it another way, as more future wealth is spent, there is a point in time where the future itself begins to look bleak rather than bright, also known as the law of diminishing returns. As you continue to spend wealth from the future today bubbles eventually become unstable as the number of available new entrants diminishes. Today the Japanese have reduced the price of new debt below zero but the problem is unsolvable. The pyramid scheme has sunk into its own unstable foundations.

The beneficiaries of the scheme have been the banks who earn interest out of nothing and established holders of assets which were funnelled into a decreasing number of hands. Because fiat money costs nothing to produce, it's just a piece of paper, it's value has been derived from convincing people to borrow, to bring forward expenditure from the future to be spent in the real economy today. Due to cui bono and hubris the banks are ploughing on, like Scott in the Antarctic, in complete denial. The bankers and their central bankers are continuing to spend the future but the future is nearly all spent. All pyramid schemes eventually fail because the earth is finite in nature.

It only takes a few devious but intelligent people to conduct a Pyramid scheme; in fact it could now be a scheme without a leader. Once the major lies are believed, such as the conflation of debt as wealth or spending as borrowing, the web is self-enforcing. I don't know who is complicit or ignorant but the entire financial system, and the mainstream media charged to protect it, is predicated on these deceits .So now you are awake and it's time to reassess, the spell has been broken, the mists have cleared. How is it possible to look at the financial system in the same way again?

Does James Murdoch's return herald a fresh £14bn bid for full control of Sky?

30 Jan 2016 11:18

The mainstream media is suffering from a collective mental illness, a state of denial, just like an alcoholic or heroin user, addicted, unable to confront the reality of the situation. They can't talk about fiat money; they can't form an argument in defence, because a ponzi scheme is a confidence trick, predicated on deceit and impossible to defend against scrutiny once exposed.

Nobody likes to admit they've been conned but pleading ignorance and retreating to a safe space hoping the problem will go away is delusional and child-like. With the truth hiding in plain view it's time for the mainstream media to front up, behave like adults, so that capitalism can get back on a sustainable course.

Rent bills high enough to make any student rebel

30 Jan 2016 17:04

Goldman Sachs and Blackstone could give crooked bankers a bad name, they like their prey captured, domesticated and dumb.

The readers' editor on... handling comments below the line

31 Jan 2016 10:12

Steven Pritchard wants everyone in a cage of their own cognizance, marked "thought criminal", beholden only to his view of the world, a tyranny of the human mind.

Google's low tax rate stretches our patience, and Osborne's crowing stretches credulity

31 Jan 2016 12:52

They say everyone has business and desires of their own - the problem with monopoly merchants, such as Google, is that they are all just crooked and dark. They get away with it for the same reason why Andrew Neil is the perfect political presenter, both are hideously ugly and morally corrupt.

What volatile markets say about the world economy

1 Feb 2016 11:55

Western Democracy stands at a crossroads and decisions have to be made. Down one road lies sustainable free market capitalism, the best price discovery and asset allocation method ever, down the other lies a corrupt, authoritarian banking tyranny, modern day robber barons and their debt serfs.

These roads are not illusions, taking the right road requires nothing but a love of your children and nature, in full cognizance of the fact that a reality adjustment for some asset bubbles is necessary to reinstate a sustainable course. Think of It like the heroin addict going cold turkey, it may sound daunting but in only a few weeks you'll be free.

The dark road consists of the slow, painful death of liberty for you and your children, the debt slaves, whose lives are being monetized, from cradle to grave, existing only to pay rent, owning nothing and loving even less. The banking tyranny is nearly complete, the debt pyramid scheme of fiat money is 40 years old and nicely funnelling real wealth to the elites at the expense of the present and future generations, but now the full take down of democracy has been planned. Real negative interest rates already exist, appropriating around 2% of your bank balance by stealth each year, but being rolled out, from Sweden to Japan, is negative nominal rates, followed by compulsory confiscations (bail-ins), abolition of cash transactions, all to maintain complete monetary control necessary for the Ponzi scheme of debt to survive.

Mark my words, unless you want your children to be debt slaves for a faceless banker, existing only to pay rent and debt repayments, owning nothing but resentment for being born into such misery, then go right ahead. Dark or light, the choice in every heart, is now needed to resist the scarlet emotion of greed, the banker's vitamin, and see the only enlightened path ahead.

In the past you had to withdraw your sword when entering battle, today the weapon is consent, withdraw it and the battle will be won and an entire future saved.

What's missing from newspaper coverage of migration? The migrants...

2 Feb 2016 12:25

He may well have to wear a muzzle in flagrante but Prof Greenslade deserves all the biting criticism he gets. Teaching his students how to be tame journalists and good debt slaves serves no purpose to improve humanity whatsoever.

All writing and journalism comes down to black and white so Roy needs to decide which side he's on.

The end of Twitter? Not for its users – we love this great leveller

2 Feb 2016 13:24

The idea that the elites hate Twitter is clearly nonsense and an inversion of reality - they want all the data they can get with which they can then game the great unwashed.

Just look at google, they are trying to monopolise thought itself. They want individuals to download all their minded thoughts and then allow google to do their thinking for them. If you can't see the real and present danger to this deviant plan, then I suggest you simply resist, resist, resist this dark technology and work to dismantle the google brain.

Google's Alphabet overtakes Apple as world's most valuable company

3 Feb 2016 09:47

Pass the priest please Gillie, it's in the net.

Be under no illusions, Google, is trying to monopolise "thought" itself.

They want individuals to type all their minded thoughts and desires into the computer and then allow Google to do their thinking for them. Your choices offered, your ideas supplied by the deviant algorithm, delivered not by detailed research and tireless comparison, but by the size of the profit paid.

Anybody who wants to produce such a monopoly will be a full blown sociopath or spectrum psychopath. As sure as night follows day the monopoly on your minded thoughts will be used against your interests. It has started with a predatory pricing profit funnel and ends with you surplus to requirements and usurped by the machine itself. They think that is progress, because in truth they hate society and themselves, but in fact, it would be technological tyranny and should be resisted at all cost.

The deviant Google brain needs to be dismantled.

Is stagnation the 'new normal' for the world economy?

3 Feb 2016 11:57

Mr El-Erian will not confront the truth about fiat money therefore his truth is primitive.

Everyone operates using Cui Bono but the enlightened see past naked self-interest at the wider forces at work.

Asteroid mining could be space's new frontier: the problem is doing it legally

6 Feb 2016 17:47

More evidence of "safe space" journalism, where nonsense is passed off as news. The thought funnel of acceptable truth is now so narrow the sun rises twice a day and the earth has become flat.

Hear Beyoncé's surprise new single, Formation

7 Feb 2016 10:08

Beyoncé is a true representative of the unsound fiat years, a perfect vehicle with which to roll out a creeping tyranny of dumbed down talentless public discourse, the destruction of beauty and free thought as the accepted truth is cornered by big sister in a corral of thought crimes.

The economic orthodoxy, fiat money, is unquestioned and unquestionable by economists, the perpetrators clinging bitterly, without the arguments, to a failed ideology that is being hidden in plain view, the behaviour of the tyrant.

Who will write the front page this nation needs?

7 Feb 2016 10:33

With sound money, the poor can be content, which is rich and rich enough.

Keynes helped us through the crisis - but he's still out of favour

7 Feb 2016 12:55

A thought experiment for those in debt to the pyramid scheme of money:

It only takes a simple lie to be believed for a new confidence to be made, a new black and white, a new reality constructed. All choices and decisions are binary events, aggregations of good and bad feelings; just in same way that the computer brain is made up of zeros and ones.

In the case of fiat economics, your reality has been constructed by accepting a single concept as fact, believing that "debt is good". The concept has been wrapped up and presented in the conflation that "debt is wealth".

The banks have convinced the media to promote the "debt is good" meme as accepted thought. Allow me to conduct a thought experiment. Debt is actually bad and Credit is good. These too concepts cannot co-exist, they are immiscible, they cannot both be right.
Banks are appealing to your bad side, your greed, your lust, your desires, to have now what you have yet to earn, to life outside of your natural balance, whereas advocates of sound money appeal to your good side, your reason, your balance, your love, and your empathy. As you can see the choice is in plain view, in black in white. Sound or unsound, that is the question.

Money without limit creates problems without solution. Money should be limited in nature.

Bill Clinton digs into Sanders in last-ditch pitch before New Hampshire vote

8 Feb 2016 19:44

I understand it's a bit rich to criticise US politics considering the state of play on airstrip 1, but nobody should take lessons from an impeached ex-potus, who unleashed the banks onto an unsuspecting public to rape and pillage at will, while he promoted the untruth that debt is wealth.

The lies trip so easily off his tongue, every word requires a health warning.

The five fears stalking the global banking industry

10 Feb 2016 09:44

Some friendly advice for Deutsche Bank, the "solid as a rock" analogy is quite a leap considering Germany doesn't have an army. Paper, Scissors, Stone.

Credit Suisse boss says European banking panic is overdone

10 Feb 2016 11:55

Tidjane Thiam is doing really well if you like pyramid schemes, black holes and cronyism. Like the money he sells he is fundamentally unsound making him perfect for the job. If he wasn't doing this he would plotting a massacre in some African back water.

I may have kissed a Tory, but I (probably) wouldn't marry one

10 Feb 2016 10:44

Can or Is Donald Trump the fiat banking interests?

10 Feb 2016 15:15

In the Interests of Sound Money.

Fiat money has created chaos out of order. Fiat money is inherently worthless as some central banks are proving. Sweden's Riksbank, for example, is unable to charge interest on its money and is in fact paying borrowers to borrow (-'ve rates) - what a state of affairs.

Sound money can always charge a positive interest rate. The bottom line is that if the rates for US$ reserve currency go negative, fiat money will be finally finished.

Hieronymus Bosch review – a heavenly host of delights on the road to hell

11 Feb 2016 11:11

As I have explained at length, the fiat monetary system is a classic Ponzi design, a pyramid scheme of debt, so understand that negative rates represent system failure, as the "Madoffs" are unable to find new entrants and have to resort to offering upfront incentive payments.

No Ponzi scheme can sustain outflows so Mrs Yellen, as controller of the world reserve, cannot go negative, but raising rates on a world already saturated in debt would cause waves of default. She is damned whichever way she turns, captured by the truth.

The markets will be the likely manifestation of the failure and when they have fully spoken, reverted back to a sustainable level, the world can start the truth and reconciliation process which will end with sound money, a sustainable future, limited in nature.

Only sound money can save the world from a fate worse than death, tyranny and enslavement.

Gilts plunge as interest rate rises recede

12 Feb 2016 09:38

May I clear up a few inconsistencies:

1. While using fiat money, banks runs are irrational and could only occur in the shortest of timeframes while the bank had more money printed. Bank runs happened in the past when your paper money was redeemable in something valuable, gold, and the banks couldn't cover the physical demand.

2. Gilts went up, the interest rate on them went down. This proves the author doesn't understand his guilt's, he's is all back to front.

3. At the risk of repeating myself, governments have historically built debt, they don't pay it back, meaning it gets rolled. Ignoring the moral imperative*, further borrowing cannot be afforded at higher rates.

*Government borrowing is financial paedophilia. Expecting future generations, those unable to vote, your children, to pay for your largesse today, is possibly the lowest act Government inflicts on its people. It is reprehensible and Larry Elliot is an enthusiastic supporter.

While I'm at it, the problem with the Labour party is that they would have you dig a hole and then fill it in again, construct a bridge and then use it for bombing practice, they would have you build a bike and then ban cycling - they have unproductive plans and imaginations. If they were proponents for balanced budgets and sound money they would sweep all before them, but they wont because they use redundant intellectual equipment.

Gilts plunge as interest rate rises recede

12 Feb 2016 13:56

The system is now so indebted the sensitivity to rate increases (elasticity) is at critical levels. A return to anywhere near historical median rates would cause widespread default. So, this presents a dilemma:
1. Deal with the problem, which is Fiat money and the ponzi scheme of debt.
2. Stumble on, in either denial or complicity, game all the data and all the markets, institute a complete banking tyranny and with it will go all your liberties, freedoms and aspirations.

The choice is clear, it just needs sound leadership from those who operate beyond cui bono.

Each generation should be better off than their parents? Think again

14 Feb 2016 13:55

A Counter Factual History of Time, Forging ahead with Sound Money:

The money we use encapsulates all our values, the manifestation of all our hopes, dreams and desires; it represents society's collective morality. Politicians are said to be a reflection of ourselves and they have never been held in less esteem. The world has reached a period of peak corruption in direct correlation with the use of fiat money.

Unsound fiat money corrupts and depraves everything in its path because it is based on a deception, an untruth, a confidence trick on the mind. Just like the machinery of a computer it all comes down to black and white, zero's and one's. Good money is earned, bad money is created and devised.

Fiat money is counterfeit, which is double-dutch for counter fact. Your reality has been inverted by believing a simple untruth, that debt with created money is an asset. Debt with created money is not wealth, it is a liability. That lie has permeated every crack and crevice of humanity. We have credit cards which in reality are debt cards, we have credit scores, which are actually your debt scores, you ask "will the bank give you credit?" in truth you are asking for debt, the banking system has inverted your reality, to protect the pyramid scheme, to keep your con.

Money which is created, which is unlimited in nature, is a twisted reality. Our current fiat money is a created pyramid scheme of debt; I defy you not to recognise the simple nature of its design, a classic ponzi scheme, layering debts upon debts, funnelling real wealth upwards into a decreasing number of hands, an inversion of trickle down.

Fiat money is debt. The key point is that fiat money is a forgery, it is created not earned. It is a public deception. It is like a construction containing a pyramid shaped keystone, placed incorrectly, liable to slip at any moment, bringing the structure crashing down.

Money which is limited in nature emits sound waves through society and is the only solution to ensure a sustainable future.

The Leveson inquiry isn't over, Cameron must keep his promise

15 Feb 2016 12:08

The PM has become so disconnected that he was recently asked "What comes before a fall?" and he replied "usually a hunt saboteur".

I wanted to say that his unjustified overconfidence is a condition entirely typical of a private school education, but that would reveal the purpose of state education is too promote under confidence in the proles.

Crime, terrorism and tax evasion: why banks are waging war on cash

15 Feb 2016 18:55

Another child-like summary of the issues at hand. Paul Mason and the BBC's Kamal Armed remind me of a Judas Goat, leading the lambs to the slaughter.

The superhero of artificial intelligence: can this genius keep it in check?

16 Feb 2016 09:33

The DEVIANT GOOGLE BRAIN is a real and present danger to humanity. As sure as night follows day this will be used against your best interests to monopolise and enslave.

Machines do not do individualism, but if you like a flat-earth, one world government, presiding over a giant financial Ponzi scheme with your purpose as a serf being usurped by the machine, to the point where you are surplus to requirements, go ahead down the dead end your being driven, although I would recommend reading Plato's Allegory of the Cave first.

RIP BBC3: from cutting-edge shows to tasteless lows

16 Feb 2016 10:10

I highlight the BBC for criticism because it generally leads the media agenda due to its monopolistic background, having been spawned from Government.

Unlike the prisoner's in Plato's Allegory of the Cave, be under no illusions. The BBC has over time, taken this principle and twisted it into today's deviant mainstream propaganda. By projecting dumbed down, narrow minded nonsense at the prisoner, sorry viewer, the collective mind of the UK has become soft and acquiescent, unquestioning and docile like cattle. The BBC, the prison guards, desire this outcome to prevent the financial pyramid scheme being questioned and exposed, the unsound fiat money and the consequences it sows.

History tells us that this is the road to tyranny, so any reduction in the BBC's output is a victory for humanity and the sustainability of our great nation.

Is the banking industry about to have its 'Uber moment'?

16 Feb 2016 11:42

The fiat model is listing; it has been holed under the surface from torpedoes of truth. The ship can't get back to shore, it is destined to sink. We need to think of a way of letting them out without drowning. The central banks, and the gatekeepers, like the BBC, are on the run, worried about the consequences of turning back to the light, riddled with doubts that they themselves will be held responsible. This is understandable but we must forgive them as most of them don't know what they've done. The outcome is the goal not the persecution of past wrongdoing.

A truth and reconciliation commission is needed to reinstate sound money and make the debt valuable again. All concerned must be invited.

Ban on Israel boycotts denies us the freedoms we say we're defending

16 Feb 2016 15:33

History has taught the PM that some people, particularly some Jews, are predisposed to manipulate and deceive their fellow human beings making them targets for bad feeling and resentment. In high ticking a certain group he is signalling a dangerous precedent, that "thought crime" exists, that you're not allowed to act on your own free will, and only he is allowed make the decisions on what's right and wrong. In short, it is the thought process of an aspiring tyrant.

Challenging the mindset of potential domestic abusers could save lives

17 Feb 2016 12:33

Most people in the UK were brought up playing Snakes and Ladders, the game based on morality where the biggest snake or vice was DEBT. Since the banks where given free reign to invert reality by promoting the myth that debt is good, the game is now known as The Battle of the Snakes.

The shills, like Paul Mason, who bark for this monopolist plutocracy seem blind to the inevitable consequences which will be complete tyranny and enslavement.

Prince William speaks out against Brexit? Rubbish

17 Feb 2016 13:19

The law of probability states that if you give a monkey a typewriter, in only an hour, it will have produced a legible string of characters, also known as words. Having read The Guardian today you might want to pass this suggestion to the editor Mr White.

OECD calls for less austerity and more public investment

18 Feb 2016 10:28

When all the fog of bluff and bluster clears all they have left is BORROW (print), BORROW (create) MORE, BORROW (print) MORE MORE.

The OECD is like a dog chasing its tail, fully unhinged, desperate to keep the con alive, desperate to keep the pyramid scheme growing, yet fully aware that they have spent all hope in the future, just too continuing living in denial today.

The Sun gives both barrels to Prince William

18 Feb 2016 12:21

The inverted images projected onto the wall of Rupert Murdoch's mind must be truly horrific if he thinks there is upside in going after the son of the future King.

The truth behind China's exchange rate delusion

18 Feb 2016 14:33

Central planning and rigged markets do not work in anything other than the shortest of timeframes. Unsound, unlimited fiat money has already caused at least one Chinese downfall and we are being driven down the same road at dangerous speeds.

I don't like fighting with the pope, said Donald Trump. And we believe him

19 Feb 2016 19:08

Very interesting Marina, the truth has a habit of focusing the mind, I suppose that's why some go to such lengths to conceal it.

Donald Trump represents a potential reset of the failed political and monetary experiments of recent years. He is putting The Federal Reserve in a corner.

Negative rates and a Fed audit has the ability to invert the pyramid, turning the famous Fed Put into a Fed Call, a huge seller hanging over the market, like the Sword of Damocles.

Cameron's deal is the wrong one: but Britain must stay in Europe

20 Feb 2016 17:39

The out campaign have got off to an inauspicious start. The "gang of six" cons include a rake, a rogue, a roaring squire, a misnomer, and a couple with the mind to create bedlam. Not a good advert.

Martians, bells, cutlery… things are all relative when you think about it

21 Feb 2016 11:11

David may have rightly highlighted The Allegory of the Cave, that things are just projections onto the cave wall of the mind.

Today, Plato would see instantly that the cave is a debtors prison. The prison guard is the bank who tells the world that debt is good, an inversion of historical truth, that a mortgage, isn't the bankers wages until death, from the French "mort" and "gage".

UK bank pay and bonuses in the spotlight as results season starts

21 Feb 2016 12:29

I wonder if the guardian know that the banks see the mainstream media as convicts with special privileges who help run the debtors prison?

Hillary Clinton needs hope and change. Can she accept that before it's too late?

21 Feb 2016 18:37

All hope has been spent with unsound money and huge budget deficits, added to which they say you can't teach an old dog new tricks so Hilary will be unable to change her bark.

HSBC 'taking too long to tackle financial crime'

22 Feb 2016 09:07

They say they're "not making enough progress on financial crime", what they mean is they are not progressing with theirs fast enough. In other words, when you have a licence to print money, backed by nothing but the misery of future generations, the panopticon debtors colony is not yet fully secure.

Money without limit causes problems without solution.

Play nice! How the internet is trying to design out toxic behaviour

22 Feb 2016 22:42

Be under no illusion, the BBC, and their acolytes, think they are your master, like a firefly trapped in a cage of their making. It wouldn't be so bad if they had a sound moral compass but they are a den of inequity, promoting deviance at every turn, including panopticon technology such Facebook etal, pyramid scheme fiat money and minority interests over that of the majority.

Richest fifth in the UK worse off since financial crash, official figures reveal

23 Feb 2016 13:13

A clumsy pastiche concealing the worst excesses of cronyism and hypocrisy lurking within a government quango.

Inside Oakwood prison: the private jail struggling to prove bigger is better

23 Feb 2016 14:25

Copying the failed model of the Americans, building a prison industrial complex, which demands more and more "customers", is tantamount to mutually assured destruction.

Carney: Bank of England could cut interest rates to zero, but not below

23 Feb 2016 15:42

Mark Carney has been a failure on every conceivable level apart from protecting the failed experiment of fiat money devised by the top tier banks, extend and pretend.

He is approaching the dishonour of Japan's Kuroda.

Happy birthday, Shelter – sadly you are needed more than ever

25 Feb 2016 12:58

Some people think this paper and the BBC is just a propaganda unit for a globalist paedophile cult with tyranny on its mind, acting on behalf of the banking cartel to infect the world with debt using unlimited fiat money. It sounds far-fetched, but on closer inspection it's clear that is the road we are being driven down.

If you support the use of fiat money, you are, by definition, a complicit financial paedophile, abusing those too young to vote because the entire system is predicated on borrowing wealth from future generations, never paying them back, and ensuring they will be increasingly worse off, renters, in perpetual debt.

The five golden rules of haggling. All right, let's call it four

25 Feb 2016 18:44

What a thing of joy is the English language, but your bastardisation of it is unbecoming.

Using the word "gold" as a substituted image, a conflation, for something good and valuable is incongruous with fiat money, it is an oxymoron, and reveals only your ignorance.

Mervyn King: new financial crisis is 'certain' without reform of banks

28 Feb 2016 10:00

If you want comprehensive proof the mainstream media is conducting a conspiracy against an unwitting population, just ask a question about the nature of the money we all use and they play dead, plead ignorance, or claim you're tantamount to a terrorist.

Fiat economics and the fiat money you have in your bank account, wallet or handbag is fundamentally unsound. It is unlimited in nature, printed by the banking cartel at will, corrupting everything in its purview. Only 40 years ago the $ was still convertible to gold, the note in your pocket was an IOU for a specified about of gold, today the $ in your pocket is just an IOU on your children's future, the more of it you spend the less well-off they will be.

Try a thought experiment and ask your representatives why they have given the power to create unlimited money to the banking cartel while receiving nothing but rampant inequality and intergenerational theft.

<Fiat money is based on a lie a confidence trick, a con, that debt is valuable and desirable. This deceit corrupts and depraves everything it touches, and since the use of money is ubiquitous, it has engulfed the entire world.>

Starter home buyers could receive £141,000 windfall from taxpayers

29 Feb 2016 08:57

The Government is openly offering "freebies" for new entrants into the scheme, tantamount to Bernie Madoff offering "free holidays" for new investors. It's a sure sign of unsustainability.

Taking the plunger: Starbucks to open first store in Italy

29 Feb 2016 11:55

If the Italian's have any self-respect left they will run this globalist monopoly merchant out of town.

BBC News faces £80m cuts over the next four years

29 Feb 2016 15:35

What is the point of BBC News, if they can't tell the truth because the enemy are watching it serves no useful purpose. Might as well put lipstick on a monkey and pump out the Newspeak via subtitles.

I would rather swim in sewage than Clean for the Queen

29 Feb 2016 15:22

BJ is a gutless, knuckle dragging can-kicker who would let us descend into the fires of hell to protect his own "legacy" before addressing the real problem at hand, fiat money and the Ponzi scheme of debt.

If a moderate like Sadiq Khan shouldn't stand for London mayor, which Muslim can?

1 Mar 2016 09:24

The whole basis of the British establishment is predicated on swearing allegiance, before God, to the Monarch, who is the head of the Church of England. This principle is immiscible with the muslim faith. A muslim cannot swear allegiance to something they don't believe in, therefore they would be perjuring themselves in front of God.

Report urges end to 94 years of BBC self-regulation

1 Mar 2016 12:21

The BBC have been given ample opportunity to change but refused. The propaganda machine for the panopticon and unsound fiat money is a foul and corrupting influence and should be disbanded for the good of humanity.

The BBC have been given ample opportunity to change but refused. The propaganda machine for the panopticon and unsound fiat money and is a foul and corrupting influence and should be disbanded for the good of humanity.

Bbc-Jon Sopel is clearly hoping Trump gets JFK'd.

One thing is for certain, America is currently the safest place on earth, there is no chance of a Muslim terrorist attack on US soil in the run up to the election.

New-look Barclays: the same, but worse

1 Mar 2016 17:00

The collective mind has been poisoned by the criminal intentions of unsound fiat money and global corporatism. Barclays is a leading player.

If you're disappointed by bleak prospects and a dark future you should really arm yourself with the knowledge of who's to blame. An entire generation has already been put to the sword as perpetual renters, scrapping by in dead end jobs, operating within the false reality of the iphone and other panopticon technology.

There comes a time in the tides of men when taken at the flood, you realise that your representatives do not have your best interests at heart. When this truth dawns alternative recourse must be sort to make the future sustainable again.

State pension age could rise faster than expected, say experts

1 Mar 2016 18:07

The system is broken, financially and morally. The "fair deal" has been replaced by a Faustian pact, to work until you drop, all because of the unsustainable debts racked up by the fiat money system and profligate politicians.

Chinese manufacturing fall adds to evidence of sharp global downturn

2 Mar 2016 09:22

The Chinese government have failed to learn from their mistakes. The fiat money system has no positive value, as negative rates all around the world testify.

Despite being the important collective feature of our lives, discussion about the way our money is organised is banned. This makes the entire foundation of society no better than an authoritarian police state.

Donald Trump marches on as Hillary Clinton sweeps south on Super Tuesday

2 Mar 2016 11:22

Donald Trump is the figurehead for sound money, liberty and good business.

The ship has set sail with supportive winds and a cargo of hope - a sustainable future for capitalism.

Bbc- Any discussion about privacy should include the Federal Reserve. Until it is audited this shadowy creature operates behind the curtain propping up markets, printing money like confetti, obfuscating the truth about fiat economics, presiding over a pyramid scheme of debt, yet accountable to nobody. It is for this reason that the financial system is an illusion predicated on corruption and deceit.

Bbc- This pseudo journalist is helping conduct a conspiracy against your financial future. The fiat money system has no positive value, as negative rates all around the world testify.

Despite being the most important collective feature of our lives, discussion about the way our money is organised is supressed. This makes the entire foundation of society no better than an authoritarian police state.

Mosul dam engineers warn it could fail at any time, killing 1m people

2 Mar 2016 12:16

Money and Religion

The way to solve the stated war on terror, the de facto religious war between Christianity and Islam, is to reinstate sound money. A compromise is needed between a full ban on interest, as required under Sharia, and fully unhinged fiat money. This could undam all the governments' problems.

In an ideal world Israel would take the lead and fly the flag for sound money. The world needs a new economic orthodoxy and leave behind the failed 40 year experiment of fiat economics. Even the name Fiat is provocative, being the reflection of Taif, the mountain range of Mecca. The whole world wants this compromise and the associated peace.

Cameron v Corbyn PMQs verdict: a Greek gift of a gag

2 Mar 2016 13:28

Just look at the way the EU have punished Greece for its flirtation with dissent last year. Not to believe a significant and sustained backlash would be inevitable, following a Brexit, is to misunderstand human nature.

BBC-Allyson Pollock thinks she is the mistress of all she surveys. She is the embodiment of the Fabian agenda to weaken everything, especially the male species, to create a grey ubiquitous pond where global socialism is your only mummy and everything is provided from that teat. To be a good debt slave you must refrain from any activity which risks injury or confrontation. If you like freedom resist.

Pensions fairness to next generation demands that we adapt to new realities

2 Mar 2016 18:58

Mr White is doing a good job, at least he's prepared to question the accepted thought evacuated by the banking propagandists.

The success of the current financial system, fiat money, is predicated on constantly increasing the amount of debt in circulation, just like a pyramid scheme. To increase debt the bank's require new entrants (debtors) and rising real asset prices. This fact makes all the old certainties redundant just to preserve this new unsustainable money system.

Eventually all pyramid schemes end, they either run out of new entrants, get exposed, or run into the limits of nature. They say it won't happen this time, but this exposes their hubris and ultimate agenda, to create a world government based on a panopticon technocracy.

Rugby Football Union accused of ignoring risks of tackling in schools

2 Mar 2016 19:42

More evidence of an out of control feminist cult member demanding to be everybody's over-bearing mummy. They want the state to trump individual responsibility.

Comprehending the depths of this agenda is just as likely to cause a headache.

MPs – don't ignore social media as the next generation of voters are watching it closely

3 Mar 2016 09:42

For the individual, Twitter and alike serves little positive purpose, but what's more concerning for humanity is that people have been conditioned to carry around their own surveillance device and prison guard of their own volition.

Every call, every stroke of the mouse, every search, every thought logged for posterity to be used against you either immediately in the marketing of over-priced goods and services, stuff you don't need, made by people you don't know, paid for with money you don't have, or, in the future, when the panopticon is fully in place, when your intelligence file is used against you. History has taught us that because monopoly power corrupts completely, such comprehensive personal information is always used to manipulate and control just like the Sarsi.

The truth is that the technocracy is designed to control and limit possibilities not expand them. For example, everyone knows that for governments, banks and big businesses, money does grow on trees. By definition fiat money, is just a piece of paper, made from pulp, with a number printed on it, but type that fact into a search engine and you are diverted into a virtual reality, a soft play area where you can remain pig ignorant.

Mark my words, the technocracy is not your friend and if you like freedom and liberty the only course of action is resistance using your own free will.

George Clooney interview: 'Donald Trump is a xenophobic fascist'

3 Mar 2016 18:24

The thing with actors is they never stop acting. They all get to a point where they don't know who they are anymore. Clooney is a case in point. His controllers have trotted him up to this because they think the public are so dumb that they will believe his drivel over a politician.

Auditing the Federal Reserve has got the establishment foaming at the mouth.

They know that when it's exposed that banks and government have created a financial pyramid scheme based on borrowing wealth from future generations, children who have no say in the matter, tantamount to financial paedophilia, the general public will be rightly repulsed.

Auditing the Federal Reserve is the first step on the road to redemption.

How extreme is a government which creates a financial system based on borrowing wealth from future generations, the children, who have no say in the matter? It is tantamount to financial paedophilia, it is the lowest act a society can conduct and is why paedophilia infected organisations like the BBC.

Auditing the Federal Reserve is the starting point on the road to redemption.

Only a new capitalism can end inequality in Britain. This is where Labour comes in

3 Mar 2016 18:38

Liam Byrne is a financial paedophile, plain and simple. He is promoting more borrowing from future generations, the children who have no say in the matter, with no intention of ever repaying. When the general public understand this fact they will be rightly repulsed. At least George Osborne wants to balance the books. Labour will never regain power unless they follow suit and adopt the principles of sound money.

Trump auditing the Federal Reserve is the first step on the road to redemption, Byrne included.

Mitt Romney says Trump's 'third-grade theatrics' not worthy of presidency

3 Mar 2016 20:02

Mitt Romney is a sign of desperation.

Audit the Federal Reserve has the dark forces rattled, they will try and rig the process, but as Victor Hugo noted, "no army can stop an idea whose time has come".

Donald Trump was supposed to lose the latest debate. Far from it

4 Mar 2016 10:10

The US establishment are petrified of Trump and **Audit the Federal Reserve**. They know Clinton is a compromised liability and will try anything to rig it against him (with electronic voting anything is possible). That said, I can confidently predict that there will be no Muslim terrorist attack in the US prior to the Presidential Election.

BBC white paper may be delayed until after EU referendum

4 Mar 2016 08:47

Given the BBC's satanic background the Government are right to be cautious handling this black sheep.

Hurrah for Spotlight and the glory of journalism! Now get me 500 words on people clapping

4 Mar 2016 10:00

The mainstream media "gatekeepers of the truth" must understand that "the average person" knows that the fix is in. Trotting up another "sentence creator" to protect the status quo just signals that their suspicions are correct.

Those in the know understand the confidence trick is fiat money and the pyramid scheme of debt.

In America, for example, the CIA spends 1/3 rd of its budget on propaganda, Hollywood films, News channel talking points, documentaries etc conditioning the masses to believe illusions like "debt is wealth" and "globalisation is in the national interest". Hollywood is a dark place.

House of Cards: a KKK connection isn't all Frank Underwood and Donald Trump share

4 Mar 2016 12:34

The Guardian trying hard to blur the lines between fiction and reality for the great unwashed.

From America to China to the Middle East general populations are beginning to see the cul de sac that successive governments , captured by the big banks and their pyramid scheme of debt, have driven them down.

I thought it was common knowledge that David Cameron privately mistrusts Dr Fox as a quisling and intellectual subordinate.

Operating cui bono in isolation reveals Theresa May as behaving like an animal marking its territory. A Home Secretary should have the ability to comprehend the bigger picture, the enlightened view, not merely a myopic desire to save her seat with cynical nimbyism.

Jeremy Corbyn's views on the sex trade sum up the male left's betrayal of women

4 Mar 2016 16:44

Another fully paid up member of the feminist cult failing for balance and accuracy. I don't care for the industry but it is conducted illegally and by adults expressing free will. Have you nothing to say about the women who make their living lying on their backs? The Treasury seem to value the industry quite a bit without material gain so it is a correct and legitimate call for legalisation, despite who made it.

Harriet Harman hits out at Corbyn's support for decriminalised sex work

4 Mar 2016 18:35

It must be a leap year, minions of the feminist cult appear howling at the moon with ill advised prejudice and hypocrisy over a legitimate idea, while in plain view the banking cartel is robbing the future blind with a pyramid scheme of debt and they couldn't care less.

School rugby-tackling ban campaigners receive 'vile' abuse

4 Mar 2016 20:05

People realise that a wider agenda is at play here, rugby being only the conduit. The censor won't let me expand on this but narrowing the Overton window of acceptable thought / ideas is central. Banning tackling is obviously a retrograde step; a regression to the lowest common denominator and all right minded individuals should resist this creeping authoritarian bent within government circles.

Mental health and debt crisis: we have to act, say thinktank founders

5 Mar 2016 10:55

These two may have good intentions but they hold a misinformed and naive understanding of the current fiat money system. They believe the banks propaganda that debt is good, debt is wealth, debt is an asset. The truth, for the borrower, is quite the opposite. Debt is only an asset, wealth and good for the bank, for the debtor, it is a liability, a yoke and bad.

The fundamental principles of fiat economics are hidden because governments have been captured by the banking cartel. It has taken only 40 years for the world to be floundering in a sea of unsustainable debt, negative interest rates just proving the fiat system is less than worthless.

The collective mind of the government is anxious, unstable and liable to continue making poor decisions, mutually assured destruction. Having spent all confidence in the future, they are yet to reach the point of acceptance, the realisation that only sound money, money which is limited in nature, can restore confidence in the future.

Make mine a large Buckie before they ban that, too

5 Mar 2016 18:18

Mr McKenna makes some interesting points. It's true to say this motley crew want everyone, including the beastly bourgeois, captured with an overton window like a split in a letterbox so that any alternative to Big Sister, unsound money, pyramid schemes of debt, perpetual war, rising inequality, cancellation of retirement, destruction of art etc etc etc is deemed too radical to even comprehend. Acceptable thought reduced to a few grunts and dribbles.

Add to the mix the deviant google and the rise of the robot and it doesn't take a great leap of faith to envisage them rolling out the "brain chips". They will spin them as "intelligent implants" but in truth they will control and deprave. The only sensible conclusion is to protect your hard won liberties at all cost whenever this rabble start foaming at the mouth.

Cruz wins Kansas Republican caucus as five states vote – campaign live

6 Mar 2016 00:15

It would be poetic justice if the Federal Reserve's bluff was Trumped.

Now the baby boomers are the reactionaries. The tables are turned

6 Mar 2016 10:10

Don't kid yourself; the baby boomers are a dishonest generation. They allowed the con men of high finance to hood wink them into believing that debt is wealth, debt is an asset, debt is good. They were, and remain, conned.

The resulting calamity is that they have already spent their children's future just to buy stuff they didn't need, made by people they didn't know, with money they didn't earn.

Can they ever be forgiven?

FCA chief denies new regime is soft on bankers

7 Mar 2016 09:25

If she wasn't fundamentally unsound she wouldn't have got the job.

Did you hear the one about Paddy Power Betfair?

7 Mar 2016 12:42

Paddy Power is a dirty protest in the face of free and fair markets open for competition. The business is now a monstrosity, like a lazy all seeing eye. As the central banks have proved unlimited power results in rigged markets. Only when the light is shone upon them will they reflect on their misdeeds. Something needs to be done as the monopoly commission is asleep on the job.

Who will care for us in the future? Watch out for the rise of the robots

6 Mar 2016 20:25

Some think the technocracy are conducting a stealth eugenics policy, but one thing is for certain, this arrangement will end in tears.

Google's artificial intelligence machine to battle human champion of 'Go'

7 Mar 2016 17:33

A thing of beauty is a joy forever, it will never fade into nothingness, and so on and so forth.

The deviant google brain will never understand the power of love.

Generation Y, Curling or Maybe: what the world calls millennials

8 Mar 2016 08:15

Who put you up to this shameless piece of deception? Hong Kong and Shanghai Bank Broadcasting Corporation. Why not do something useful and write about the causal links between fiat money - "created debt" and rampant generational and intergenerational inequality creating a new feudal system? Unless you do it's obvious to everyone your either ignorant or complicit in a cover-up.

David Hare: Why the Tory project is bust

8 Mar 2016 08:33

The Tory project is bust because it believes only in secret societies, creating monopolies and unsound money. After any period in power the Tory party cannot contain its hatred of the great unwashed, "the customers" and is repulsed by the idea of competition.

Rise in use of contraception offers hope for containing global population

8 Mar 2016 08:52

The Guardian's true condition is one of denial.

The paper won't talk about the unsound fiat money, created debt, the pyramid/ponzi scheme which needs new entrants to survive, yet, they recognise the world population trend is unsustainable.

May I suggest the paper stop thinking that this is a "con" we all benefit from, because the argument doesn't stand up to scrutiny.

Ryanair launches corporate jet service

9 Mar 2016 13:43

Paddy power's takeover of Betfair is a defenestration of its reputation as a competitive free and fair marketplace.

The Irish mafia have been conducting business in the usual manor for too long, corrupting weak and vulnerable minds with a nudge and a wink in exchange for an offshore bank account, a cheap racehorse, or a miraculous land deal. In horse racing it only takes one entry to be pulled for the book to become extremely profitable. This new business will further corrupt and deprave, not just because it's offshore, but it gives Paddy Power access to the workings of the once "free-market", like a betting panopticon, a big brother looking over everyone's shoulder. This data can then be used to further game the system.

The monopolies commission are either asleep on the beach or complicit in an agenda to destroy free markets. They should be ashamed on themselves and reverse this monstrosity immediately.

On the subject of horse racing, for me, Richard Johnson is the greatest jockey since John Francome. Honest as the day is long, he clearly loves the horses he rides, they feel it, and with his exceptional skill and judgement, the partnership becomes of one mind, running and jumping, for fun. Given a race with horses of equivalent ability RJ's would prevail every time.

ECB expected to launch new stimulus measures today - business live

10 Mar 2016 11:11

Thomas Jefferson once said that "Fiat money is a greater threat than terrorism".

Fast forward a few years and today we have Mario Draghi operating a fully unhinged, yet legal, monetary system called fiat money. Draghi is just a man with a photocopier, a smile and lots of secrets. It is economics based on a classic ponzi scheme with counterfeit money and illusions.

Who in the mainstream media has the integrity to question this fantasy economics being hidden in plain view? Why can't someone ask a simple question "If the money is free why can't I get any for my constituents or a new school or that windfarm?" That question can't be answered without revealing the money is fundamentally unsound, backed by nothing but the guaranteed poverty and inequality of future generations.

For me, this experiment with unlimited fiat money has reached peak corruption, with no credible defence, and is approaching financial tyranny dragging humanity backwards into its web of lies and deceit. It must be stopped and the principles of sound money reintroduced, money which is limited in nature.

Democratic debate: it's painful to watch Clinton and Sanders go at each other

10 Mar 2016 12:42

Warm, passionate, honest, transparent, constitutional.

Hilary Clinton displays none of these attributes; instead she sticks to the lines given to her by the Banking Cartel like superglue. She is the establishment stooge and therefore not in your best interests.

You want to stop people swearing in the posh part of town? *#?! off!

10 Mar 2016 11:55

This is just Big Sister trying to put a child lock on the Overton Window of the peasantry. They want to limit all thoughts and ideas to a few grunts and groans, like pigs in a pen.

ECB cuts interest rates and boosts QE stimulus programme - business live

10 Mar 2016 13:00

Now he's stuffing big corporations with unrepayable debt which they will use for no useful purpose. Draghi is corrupting the entire world with his unaccountable photocopier of unsound money. This bedlam is mutually assured destruction.

Mario Draghi holds press conference after ECB cuts interest rates and boosts QE - business live

10 Mar 2016 14:41

Is Deflation the only thing in the apothecary box which will make the banks take their medicine?

Labour would borrow billions of pounds to fund public investment projects

10 Mar 2016 21:49

Keep inflating the debt bubble will at best ensure the rampant inequality continues until all the real assets are owned by a tiny minority - all caused by the unsound money funnel which is fiat money. McDonnell has been hoodwinked by laziness or incompetence, either way this financial paedophile is a real and present danger to everyone bar an elite few.

Cheaper cities? Economist index shows cost of urban life is going down

11 Mar 2016 13:11

I can't agree with anything in this article. No serious economist can make debt comparisons with the pre 1973 era. Debt created with fiat money is like chalk and cheese when compared to commodity backed money, even with fractional reserve.

The more powerful the US militarily has become, the more unsound the US$ has become, a self-reinforcing spiral. You can't have unsound fiat money without a military advantage, so on so forth. We are in a brave new world predicated on lies and illusions created to protect the confidence of a ponzi scheme.

The destination on this road is total world domination and the destruction of all competing sovereign nations. Only by having independent sovereign nations can a natural limit be placed on this US expansion. Perversely, the American people aren't aware of the ambitions of the US establishment and if they did I'm sure they wouldn't support it. This makes the future unsustainable.

No serious economist can make debt comparisons with the pre 1973 era. Debt created with fiat money is like chalk and cheese when compared to commodity backed money, even with fractional reserve. The more powerful the US militarily has become, the more unsound the $ has become, a self-reinforcing spiral. You can't have unsound fiat money without a military advantage, so on so forth. We are in a brave new world predicated on lies and illusions created to protect the confidence of a ponzi scheme. The destination of this road is total world domination and the destruction of all competing sovereign nations. Only by having independent sovereign nations can a natural limit be placed on the US expansion. Perversely, the American people aren't aware of the ambitions of the US establishment and if they did I'm sure they wouldn't support it. This makes the future unsustainable.

Alastair Campbell slams 'dishonesty' of papers backing EU exit

12 Mar 2016 20:20

There is no limit to Campbell's hypocrisy. He should stick to making the pot noodles at Portland Communications.

Donald Trump Chicago rally called off amid protests and violence

12 Mar 2016 11:33

Chicago is the natural home of the gangster, where you can rent-a-mob at the City Hall.

Argos patiently waits for its buyer to collect

13 Mar 2016 11:33

The Spectre of Perma-Stagnation by Design

Free market capitalism is now but a conceptual illusion. Today we are living in a managed command and control economy under an increasingly barbaric fiat banking tyranny. The money is unlimited, unless you need it, while some governments and big business are being paid by the banks to borrow, yet savers cannot receive a real return. Any store of wealth which isn't limited in nature is destined to lose value. The debt mountain has never been bigger, every second of every day the debt is increasing, layer upon layer of new debt based money being created, unrepayable and unaccountable. Herein lies the truth that cannot be concealed.

As the fiat pyramid scheme grows, interest rates can never return to median levels. This is why inflation cannot be seen to increase. If the banker's public face, the central banks, wanted to create inflation it could be done at a stroke. In the same way that GDP figures were inflated by including estimates of illegal drugs and prostitution, the existing inflation calculation could simply include housing costs. Inflation cannot rise because this would trigger interest rate hikes. If interest rates were to rise, the mega debt would be unserviceable. The pyramid is inherently unstable when default occurs.

Those who designed pyramids of debt in full knowledge that it would be done on the backs of future generations, ensuring children will be successively worse off, while real assets are funnelled to the top, have made the ultimate Faustian pact. Only the worshipers of baphomet would plead to the weaknesses of greed, envy and loathing to satisfy their own, while feasting on the guaranteed misery of younger generations.

The current fiat system of unsound money is trapped, and its continued existence is now being engineered as a managed decline into a tyranny; society and existing liberties taken down by design. The mind-set of the bankers is Too Big to Fail, for everybody else, Too Big to Fail must be confined to the dustbin of history. Hubris, oaths or simple cui bono prevent them from changing of their own volition, they've made their deal and that is to abuse, corrupt and exploit the power to create money.

The signs are all around, the world is on course to morph into a grey wasteland with an elite plutocracy, and associated forces, presiding over a neo-peasant class extinguished of all hope in perpetual borderline poverty, surviving on a diet of emptiness, transfixed by the flicker rate, able only to muster a series of grunts from the confines of a cell provided generously by the panopticon of total surveillance. Only sound money can reverse this direction of travel.

If public trust in government is at all-time lows why would we entrust all our values to a set of unaccountable bankers who don't have our best interests at heart? This is why they must be accountable to an entity greater than themselves, the whole power of nature pitched against the weakness and fallibility of a human mind. Unsound money, created by deception, acts like a poisoned arrow on the body of society. I ask the question, who do you trust to control the money, and by definition your values, a secretive society of bankers or the physical limits afforded by nature, all those years that evolution has created? For me, these natural limits should include a basket of goods, not just gold; this would represent a true layer of accountability above the fragility of the human condition, a new money which everyone can believe in.

ExoMars: 'giant nose' to sniff out life on Mars prepares for launch

13 Mar 2016 16:07

The Universe maybe expanding but back down to earth the natural boundaries of the planet are not. Why don't these people concentrate on making life on Earth sustainable before dreaming about the darkness?

George Osborne's budget message will be: this is no time for a Boris

14 Mar 2016 10:24

George Osborne needs to prove that sound money is the destination. More can-kicking will not suffice; the "fiddling while Rome burns" can be left to BJ.

The BBC's constant promotion of job destroying technology and bigtech tax avoiders breaks it's own guidelines for impartiality.

The same one-eyed, flat-earth approach is applied to money and economics. Bitterly clinging to fiat economics while sound money is hidden from view brings the whole organisation into disrepute. The money contains all our values and yours are neither fair nor balanced.

Anyone worth, over say, $100m I find offensive. There is no limit to some people's greed.

ExoMars spacecraft sets off in search of alien life

14 Mar 2016 10:52

The Expanding Universe Scheme crowd are other worldly in their deviance and denial. If planet Earth is a cauldron it is boiling over as they add more paper to the fire. Negative real rates mean positive returns are impossible unless you take unacceptable market risks.

Facebook, Google and WhatsApp plan to increase encryption of user data

14 Mar 2016 11:42

These devices are wide open. They are secure like a school child at the BBC.

Gove 'should resign if he briefed Sun about the Queen's political views'

14 Mar 2016 18:35

Michael Gove is one desperate man, although in his defence, who wouldn't be as the alleged mistress of Ian Duncan Smith.

Alastair Campbell launches attack on SNP and Boris Johnson

14 Mar 2016 21:00

Campbell must be getting brave because he knows that Boris is also the type who relishes more time at home alone humping the furniture while barking like a dog in high heels.

Alastair Campbell launches attack on SNP and Boris Johnson

14 Mar 2016 21:42

Nicola Sturgeon is the female version of Macbeth, double double, toil and trouble, Nose of Turk, Liver of Blaspheming Jew, and so on and so forth. She is brim full of unjustified hubris yet has no comprehension about even the most rudimentary principles of fiat money and economics.

As a result she is swimming In the shallows just waiting to be caught and dispatched.

'Failing' Grayling saves Michael Gove's blushes in Queen Brexit row

14 Mar 2016 23:03

Grayling is fragile like a bull in China's shop.

George Osborne's recovery is in danger: the only option now is to steal Jeremy Corbyn's clothes

15 Mar 2016 09:44

As the media continue its primary role of silencing all critics of fiat money, it is only fair that the socialists now have their day. The old argument goes that "socialism always fails because it always runs out of other people's money". This was Pravda. Today it is clearly nonsense.

Under fiat economics, the money flows like wine from the photocopier, unaccountable and unhinged. Draghi doesn't borrow he prints, the socialists are now right, money is no object, it is free, unlimited like the Universe. All problems have been solved, Draghi etal have promised "whatever it takes" and never forget, their word is their bond.

Lib Dems attack 'gutless' Labour over surveillance bill

15 Mar 2016 12:21

Be under no illusion, everyone is under suspicion, everyone is a potential threat. The surveillance state panopticon is only a step away from the internment camps.

Is Osborne afraid to tell us the budget's impact on family incomes?

15 Mar 2016 15:40

Any talk of "savers" is an insult to everybody's intelligence. Fiat money destroys, by design, the fortunes and principle of "saving". With negative real rates, it is just a question of much your going to lose.

Chuka Umunna in radio spat with Boris Johnson over Brexit stance

15 Mar 2016 18:10

The ex Home Secretary is only throwing around dead cats as a diversion.

Theresa May's tyrannical power grab of liberties in the Total surveillance Bill is unprecedented in its breadth. Now every Council worker with a grudge will be able to access your innards and use this information as power to control. Bribery and extortion is set to sky-rocket.

Elon Musk by Ashlee Vance review – how one tech billionaire plans to save the world

16 Mar 2016 09:44

Musk is the classic predatory sociopath who understands the fiat ponzi scheme and embraces it for his own ends while plotting a shuffle from the Mortal Coil. If he had any light in his heart he would use his intelligence to stop Yellen and the Federal Reserve in their tracks. The limits of planet Earth demand sound money, limited in nature, as Victor Hugo said, "no army can stop an idea whose time has come."

BBC Breakfast seating bias due to 'misogyny', says ex-Countryfile host

16 Mar 2016 10:44

The foul air evacuated by the BBC flicker rate is steeped in deviant neuro programming with the intention of suppressing logical right thinking with the primary intention of getting the populous to believe the bankers con, the inversion, that debt is good, saving is bad, and pyramid schemes of unlimited debt don't create rampant intergenerational inequality and a money funnel to a diminishing number of real asset holders.

Nine councils defy the government by publishing their own papers

16 Mar 2016 13:07

My Liedar is flashing red for danger.

Narrowing the main stream of information, just like the money funnel, increases system volatility because distortions make reversion to the mean more violent. The entails of tyranny are worn around Pickle's neck.

Dovish Yellen cheers markets ahead of Bank of England rate decision - business live

17 Mar 2016 09:44

I trust a lump of silver, gold or any other fruit of nature, more than Janet Yellen, and all other central bankers, every, every, every time.

Fiat money corrupts everything in its path because it requires lies, diversion and deceit to maintain the confidence in it. Want proof? Then see how all discussion of the money is suppressed, like an establishment paedophile enquiry, by the mainstream media.

So Theresa May has breasts – who knew?

17 Mar 2016 13:57

I presume it was just a cynical diversion to get the tame journalists foaming at the mouth, but it either way, her owner should be made aware of the new Dangerous Dogs Act.

What Donald Trump's butler saw: behind the scenes of a real-life Xanadu

17 Mar 2016 18:44

The author's thinly veiled hate of Trump has tainted her usual ability to string lovely words together in a thought provoking way. Love trumps hate every, every, every time.

US confidence data disappoints, while ECB hints at helicopter cash –
as it happened

18 Mar 2016 10:42

This pronouncement has opened up a gaping rift between the ECB
and the BBC.

The BBC claim, as referenced by last night's Newsnight, that fiat
money is not infinite. Mr Praet's helicopter money flatly contradicts
this. The 2 positions are immiscible, they both can't be correct, so,
the questions is, who is right, the BBC or the ECB?

We dreamed of teleportation. We got self-lacing shoes

18 Mar 2016 21:12

Before Classics was removed from the Comprehensive syllabus,
even the Proles, like myself, knew about Narcissus, that mirrors
showed the soul, reflecting stored memories and hiding the guilty
conscience. If people today spent more time comprehending these
elements of the dark side they would think twice about the selfie
stick, put down their camera phones and educate themselves
quickly in the ways of the world, otherwise they will be robbed of
any future as renters, in perpetual debt, without chance of parole.

The unlimited money pyramid scheme, called fiat money, is not
being run for their benefit, and that is why you never hear anything
about it even in The Guardian.

Yes, he tried: what will Barack Obama's legacy be?

19 Mar 2016 14:14

For me, Obama's legacy will be
"Logic is an enemy, Truth is a menace, and Reason is a national

security risk."

(Oh, and don't mention the infinite $**Debts**) America is regressing before our eyes.

Duncan Smith attacks 'unfair' budget in first interview since resigning

20 Mar 2016 11:22

Love, Loyalty and Stamina, IDS displays none of these characteristics.

This is about the crisis within Governments regarding Central banking. With their "unlimited" money they pick the deserving and undeserving, giving handouts to rich friends while throwing scraps into the gutter for the poor.

This is why the BBC and ECB are at war over the question "Is the supply of fiat money infinite?". The BBC is about to U-turn, and admit that fiat money is infact unlimited.

The whole fiat system is predicated on borrowing from the next generation, those unable to vote, with no intention of repaying.

Tories in civil war as Duncan Smith attacks austerity programme

20 Mar 2016 10:57

Clearly IDS can't take the lies surrounding the BBC/ECB anymore.

The current "Fiat money" is created, not owed or accountable, it is unlimited and pretending otherwise is fundamentally dishonest.

That is why the important financial news is the day is the rift between the BBC and the ECB.

The BBC claim that fiat money is not infinite. Yesterday The ECB'S

Mr Praet discussed "helicopter" or "confetti" money which flatly contradicts the BBC. The 2 positions are immiscible, they both can't be correct, so, the questions is, who is right, the BBC or the ECB?

Why is the BBC continuing to propagate "lies"?

SXSW: 'It's pretty much the same mess it was last year'

20 Mar 2016 16:38

Because the entire system is built on a farrago of lies, the truth is almost always the opposite of that portrayed by the mainstream media.

This piece of work is a case in point.

Osborne's weakness suddenly becomes a big headache for Cameron

20 Mar 2016 17:37

Ignoring the fact that the entire economy is an inflated bubble of debt, any government who runs a budget deficit, with no intention of repaying, is running a scheme tantamount to economic paedophilia. The economic orthodoxy is now so narrow and warped, the hacks like Mr Elliot are getting castled by the truth on a daily basis, making them look greedy, ignorant and corrupt.

Trump says 'professional agitators' are to blame for violence at rallies

20 Mar 2016 18:42

In the lonely desert of the human experience, some things lift us above the stones of the earth and pigs of the field. Today that thing is Donald Trump.

Audit the Federal Reserve will break the Banking Cartel from the inside, and in a stroke, make America great again with a sound $ everybody can believe in.

The majority of people operate with naked cui bono and seek to protect their assets at all costs. This makes the job of enlightening people to the path of sound money harder.

BBC Radio 4 cleared over sexually explicit Fear of Flying adaptation

21 Mar 2016 11:34

The BBC is doing a good job of telling people the wrong way to think.

They will continue to plumb new depths because their base premise is predicated on a deception. Despite admissions from the ECB last week the BBC still refuse to admit that fiat money is unlimited. It is like denying that the sun rises in the east and sets in the west.

The fiat money system is based on a farrago of lies, and the BBC are propagating them. If they can't accept the truth they will be castled by it.

George Osborne made 'mistake' over disability cuts, says Boris Johnson

22 Mar 2016 11:33

Mark Carney and Mario Draghi keep telling everybody that the money is unlimited, created at will, infinite bank bailouts, deficit financing and helicopter drops, whatever it takes to maintain the system.

That being the case, why can't an MP ask George Osborne: "if the money is unlimited, why are you cutting budgets and persecuting the poor and disabled?".

The question is simple, honest and factually correct. Failure to ask it would signify that the democratic process conducted in the Houses of Parliament is just an illusion, a charade which should be disbanded.

Disability benefits U-turn 'will add £1.3bn a year to welfare budget'

22 Mar 2016 17:08

Robert Chote is a professional liar who knows very well that the money is infinite and unlimited. The government trying to claim the high moral ground over this u turn is like a prison guard saying "your lucky we're feeding you".

Sports Direct's Mike Ashley proves silence isn't always golden

22 Mar 2016 21:55

As Mike Ashley knows, the supporter led consortium, along the lines of the Bayern Munich model, is waiting patiently in the wings for circumstances to arise and talks to begin.

Fans all around the world, from MP's to footballing royalty, are wishing and hoping for this new dawn to release Newcastle United from the icy grip of greed, cui bono and exploitation. Only then can this once great club regain the true support and heights it deserves.

If you really want to see class war, look at the warring Tories

23 Mar 2016 09:13

Yesterday's last minute, "nothing to see here", exclusion of poppers/amyl nitrate from the psychoactive substances Bill tells you everything you need to know about the vacuous depths of politicians. Making policy on the hoof to appease her "friend" Crispin Blunt, at the expense of the facts proves cronyism is flourishing under this Home Secretary. Theresa May is making a mockery of out of logic and reason, this Government needs to be attacked with the full force of the truth.

We welcomed refugees in 1945. We can't abandon them today – video

23 Mar 2016 10:15

I'm terribly sorry Mr Smith I can't agree with your 1945 comparison. The Government starts the wars, which cause the refugees, which builds the resentment and the strength of the counter forces. The Government let in military aged enemy combatants under the cover of refugees. The enemy combatants attack their targets. It is tantamount to letting the enemy attack. The ignorance, stupidity and sheer hubris of the decision making is staggering which leads to the conclusion that wider, darker agendas are at play.

The Muslim faith is immiscible with liberal Western "pseudo capitalism". They want to live under Sharia Law, banning interest on money, with medieval illiberal attitudes. The media defend these views which leaves them and their hypocrisy in contempt.

The whole experiment of mass migration has been a disaster for the West. The wider agenda is globalisation, the desire for one world government under a fiat banking cartel. The fiat pyramid scheme demands more customers at every juncture and immigration provides these new debt slaves to keep the bubble growing. It's obvious to everyone either the unsustainable debt bubble bursts or global fiat economics is a fast lane to one world government and total tyranny. In truth, our politicians are leading us on the road to hell.

We welcomed refugees in 1945. We can't abandon them today – video

23 Mar 2016 11:22

The state of modern Britain. When the censor hates the truth, when you know you're being driven down the road to hell, when all the lemmings shout "you're a fool, don't go", what is the honest man supposed to do?

Labour's challenge: to rescue capitalism from its own arrogance

23 Mar 2016 17:50

Mr White, playing dumb may fool most of the crockles but I believe you do actually understand the rudiments of fiat economics. The current "Fiat money" is created, not earned, owed or accountable, it is unlimited and pretending otherwise is fundamentally dishonest. Draghi is creating 100bn Euro a month for his pets.

Capitalism using fiat money is a misnomer; it is money funnel crony capitalism at best, a fast lane to economic enslavement and tyranny at worst. It would be shame for you to be known as another professional liar who knows very well that the money is infinite and unlimited yet chooses to mug the general public instead.

The forgotten genius: why Anne wins the battle of the Brontës

23 Mar 2016 20:00

I find the hypocrisy surrounding media feminists highly objectionable. Hidden in plain view, Muslim woman in the mainstream of that faith are treated like 2nd class citizens, covered, restricted and supressed. How can that be compatible with the feminist agenda of equality? In not questioning these clearly illiberal views the feminist cause is dragged down to that of a one-eyed, flat earth cult, completely disconnected from reality.

God Is No Thing by Rupert Shortt review – an excellent response to New Atheism

24 Mar 2016 10:10

In the face of the Devil the Church has become a "wee timorous cowering beastie", a mouse hoping the big fat cat will go away. It has taken only 40 years for the Church to fully succumb to the banker's poison, greed, to the point today where it is morally redundant, operating only as ceremonial cover and a property hedge fund. In fact, Islam has trumped Christianity as a religious force meaning The Islamic State of Britain is a distinct possibility even in the reign of the Queen.

The moral of the story is that if you allow "the money" to become unsound so will the morals of the people who use it. Fortunately it's not too late for the Church, and indeed you Mr Williams, to have a Road to Damascus moment, to repent and throw off the bankers chains. It can all be done in a few words, debt is not good, fiat money is bad.

Media organisations should be forced to publish comprehensive diversity data

25 Mar 2016 10:28

The establishment today has a similar look to failing regimes of the past. As Mark Twain noted history doesn't repeat itself but it certainly rhymes. Just one look around the corridors of power and the influence of secret societies and religious groupings is again too strong. One of the most dominant is the Jewish faith in the media. The mainstream media in the UK consists of only a handful of outlets which pump out the talking points of government and the intelligence services delivered by editorial guidance and group think. This media acts as gatekeepers of "acceptable thought and ideas".

Understandably in reaction to the atrocities of the Nazi's, Jews organised and made informed and conscious decisions to prevent history from rhyming by controlling the narrative in relation to those events and the Jewish faith more generally. But, because Jews hold their religion over nationhood, they are Jewish before British; they have promoted their own, in pursuit of power, so quickly they have built up a disproportionate influence, so that today the UK media can be considered a propaganda wing. The BBC is the case in point.

The problem is that an inherent defensiveness and paranoia has resulted in a narrowing Overton window, preferring to shut down new ideas rather than confront them, turning blind eyes when it's inconvenient, such as in banking and the fraud of unsound fiat money. A truly representative voice of Britain can't be heard until equality of opportunity is promoted and concentrations of power disbanded.

Russia criticises Amber Rudd over 'misleading' gas export comments

25 Mar 2016 15:27

You can tell when she's lying because her mouth moves.

Hadley Freeman: in Donald Trump's world, you're classy or a loser. Which is he?

26 Mar 2016 10:58

Nobody likes a hypocrite, unless you're the establishment, or mainstream media, in which case you're a perfect "type", being eminently corruptible and fundamentally unsound.

This writer is happy to endorse a financial system, which has in a generation enslaved the future to that of "renters" and "debt slaves", with social mobility and opportunity sacrificed on the altar of a satanic pyramid scheme of debt, yet Trump, who has the wherewithal to reverse this experiment, is castigated in her web of ignorance. This "slam the front door, I'm ok jack attitude" is the perfect advertisement for a society regressing before our eyes.

BBC will find it hard to shake off guiding hand of government

27 Mar 2016 11:34

I object to the BBC on many levels, it is unrepresentative, hypocritical with an agenda I find highly offensive, yet I am obliged to fund them. No matter who's winning smile or pretty ankle they get to front the action, the playbook is dark, using group think to promote everything from ponzi scheme money to the technocracy and one world government. Everything they do is designed to break the individual's free will, through the manipulation of the flicker rate.

I recently challenged them to a £1,000,000 bet that I could, in 1yr, form a rowing squad off the streets which could beat the Oxbridge Boat Race winner, male or female. Of course they declined without a response (we can't have it known that we're ruled by the least among us). Unless you're prepared to lie about the fact that the money we use is unlimited and fundamentally unsound, you're not welcome at the home of inverted reality, the Ministry of Truth.

These Tory messages show us why faith has no place in politics

27 Mar 2016 19:22

You need a lot of faith in the power of the state to have confidence in unlimited fiat money.

Kremlin accuses foreign parties of Putin smear campaign before elections

28 Mar 2016 20:44

If I were advising Mr Putin I'd suggest imposing a natural limit on personal wealth, such as no individual being worth over say $1bn. In a stroke this would rearrange priorities in the councils of government and set a precedent of restraint and altruism, the most noble of causes. Even with $1bn he may feel poorer, but content, which is rich and rich enough.

The 'invisible hand' won't save the British steel industry. State aid can

30 Mar 2016 17:44

When Adam Smith talked about the" invisible hand of the market" society was using good, sound money, commodity money, limited and backed by gold. At the same time the phase "throwing good money after bad" was coined.

Today both phases have been inverted because the market now uses unsound money, unlimited, in effect, bad money. The result of passing bad money is that the market has also gone bad and the invisible hand of the market now represents "the devil", "satan" or "darkness" which ever you prefer.

Until you understand the nature of the money we use, everything will appear inverted, perverse and confusing.

England frustrated as Luciano Narsingh goal seals Holland's comeback

30 Mar 2016 09:39

It didn't help that the crowd looked mesmerised by the zombie flicker rate of those deviant advertising boards. Wembley really is just a corporate viper's pit.

Financial traders clash over plans to build masts higher than Shard

31 Mar 2016 21:21

These parasites provide no benefit to the functioning of a free and fair marketplace and are merely symptomatic of the rigged exchanges in this era of central bank omnipotence. They will claim they provide liquidity but this is an illusion just like their order books. All intelligent people will agree this market abuse needs to be stopped forthwith.

The BBC is too timid. Being impartial on the EU is not enough

1 Apr 2016 10:38

Everybody knows the fake journalists at Sky and Channel4 are just dark propagandists for their banking and global mega-corporation owners, but the BBC should be different.

Standards have slipped so far that tame BBC journalists are just proselytizing like late stage entrants to an Ann Summers Convention, totally unaware they are propping up a Ponzi scheme.

Britain's free market economy isn't working

If Britain had an honest look in the mirror it would find that, despite a tenuous control of the language, we are really no better than America, an empty vessel, fallen from grace. Today the aging Anglo-American establishment lead the world only in propagating financial fraud, the marketing of tricks and games, and the promotion of unlimited pyramid scheme money.

The lies, deceptions and illusions produce "leaders" like Obama and Cameron who drain all hope from the hearts of the population, merely representing the agents and advertising spivs, the conmen and manipulators, who on our screens, tempt the mind and lead the eye with dark and devious intentions, the distributors of poison flour; and all predicated on the belief that ordinary people, the animals, are to be exploited and farmed like domestic cattle. What a state of affairs.

The 100 best nonfiction books: No 10 – The Selfish Gene by Richard Dawkins

The "nature of the money" is the root from which the tree of society grows. If you're interested, the tree looks weak, lanky and top heavy, vulnerable to a storm, because it's rooted in foundations of sand.

4 Apr 2016 12:22

Cui bono is the reason people like Prof Dawkins won't address the issue de jour- unlimited fiat money and the pyramid scheme of debt.

Only revolutionary ideas will shake loose the future from the grasping hands of the established order. The status quo is in a battle against time. They know that as fewer people are able, or convinced, to join the Ponzi scheme, the pyramid itself becomes less stable because more people have the self-interest to destroy it. This means government will become more authoritarian to reduce the risk of being flooded by a wave of disenfranchised citizens.

So "journalists" who think they can play dead because it's a ponzi scheme they benefit from should think again because the future is creeping up fast and it isn't going to be friendly.

Conclusion

Even after a year of effort I have failed to get a simple question such as "is the money we use unlimited?" answered by the mainstream media. It proves just how narrow the stream of acceptable discord is and why control of the "media" is such an important and prized asset. You can have all the free speech you like so long as it coincides with that of the censor, everything else considered a thought crime; it's tantamount to an intellectual tyranny. When ideas are supressed it's a tacit admission that they contain a truth that is too powerful to contain.

The control of the narrative is the attraction and purpose of the media and explains why ownership is such a prized asset, worth considerably more than the face value of profitability. The real value of newspapers, despite being mostly unprofitable, lies in the minds of the readership, building trust and telling them the right things to worry about, the right way to think. Add to the mix a real conspiracy worth hiding, such as the nature and consequences of fiat money, and then the power to sculpt the talk points such as "debt is good" and "the money is sound", represents real leverage and power for the owner. As I've said before it only takes a handful of dedicated and influential hands to run a confidence game, to invert of the truth, a con, especially one which appeals to short term greed, like fiat money.

Most "journalists" are unaware they are effectively under this mind control, conditioned to spout the lies, which is the real power of propaganda. If you've told a lie often enough, from a plausible source, without external contradiction, the innocent mind will undoubtedly believe it. This is the state of the mainstream media today, in blunt, a conspiracy against you and your children, a sea of ignorance, pumping out the talking points unaware they themselves are also being conned by the wicked inversion of truth.

Nothing important was ever likely to be changed without significant resistance, the vested interests in control of the money have limitless financial reserves but they lack the truth which is the fatal flaw in their arguments. True liberty can only exist when using sound money. If Government could restore this freedom, it would also restore faith in itself, an outcome which only a tiny minority would resist.

As Victor Hugo said "No army can stop an idea whose time has come." Sound money, money which is limited in nature, is that idea, and I'm wishing and hoping that its time has come. I will continue making the case, confident that to make is to believe, and persist in appealing to logic, reason, and truth, so once more, the light of liberty will shine again.